NEAR THE BORDER

BY THE SAME AUTHOR

Poetry
Lives
The Caught Sky
The Flower Industry
Brushing the Dark
Album of Domestic Exiles
Russian Ink
The Islanders
The Unmapped Page – Selected Poems
Tremors – New & Selected Poems
Speed & Other Liberties
Fuel
The Lives and Times of the Islanders
The Bicycle Thief & Other Poems
Baffling Gravity

Essays
How to Proceed
The Hallelujah Shadow

Anthologies
First Rights – a Decade of Island Magazine (with Michael Denholm)
Toads

NEAR THE BORDER

New & Selected Poems

ANDREW SANT

© Andrew Sant 2023

This book is copyright. Apart from any fair dealing for the purposes of study and research, criticism, review or as otherwise permitted under the Copyright Act, no part may be reproduced by any process without written permission. Inquiries should be made to the publisher.

First published in 2022

Published by Puncher and Wattmann
PO Box 279
Waratah NSW 2298

http://www.puncherandwattmann.com
poetry@puncherandwattmann.com

A catalogue record for this book is available from the National Library of Australia

ISBN   9781922571793

ABOUT THE AUTHOR

Andrew Sant was born in London in 1950. He emigrated in 1962 with his parents to Melbourne where he completed his formal education. He has lived in London at various times, particularly during the last decade. During this period he has been a Writing Fellow at the Universities of Leicester, Chichester, London (Goldsmiths College) and Kent. In 2001 he was writer in residence in Beijing, China at the University of Peking. In 1979 after moving to Hobart he co-founded the Tasmanian-based literary quarterly *Island* and served as joint editor for a decade. He has worked as a teacher of literacy to prisoners and the unemployed, of English to non-English speakers and of humanities subjects to students in mainstream institutions. He has also been a copywriter and a manager of a hostel for juvenile offenders. He is a former member of the Literature Board of the Australia Council. His essays have appeared in the annual *Best Australian Essays* anthologies, and two collections *How to Proceed* and *The Hallelujah Shadow* were published in 2016 and 2020 respectively. His poems have been widely anthologised. In 2003 he was awarded the Centenary Medal.

CONTENTS

from LIVES (1980)

Lives	3
Milking Three Cows at Nightfall	4

from THE CAUGHT SKY (1982)

The Geologist in a Cave	7
The Optometrist	8
The Short Cut	9
Glenlyon	11
Through the Panama	12
The Shoe Repairer	14
Fancy Dress	15
The Fear	17
Wren	18
Westbrooke Banks	19
Convict Settlement, Saltwater River	20
Literacy Lessons	21
1 *A Class of Unemployed Youth*	
2 *The Improver*	
from Rural Episodes	23
Duel	
Blackberries	
The Resort	25
Homage to the Canal People	26
Northwood Hills	27
Morning in Oslo	28
A Sense of Loss	29
Westminster Incident	30
Moss	31
Myrtle Forests	32
Old Woman in Apple Country	33
Trails	34

from THE FLOWER INDUSTRY (1985)

Soundwaves	37
Fires	39
1 The Observer	
2 The Volunteer	
The Reason for Fires	41
Tremors	43
from Strategies and Rehearsals	45
The Bank Robbers	
A Game of Golf	
The Fat Man as Nudist	
A Protest Song	48
Driving through Connemara	49
The Behaviour of Plover	50
Reading for Pleasure	52
The Flower Industry	54
Elegy for Shoes	55
Origin of the Species	56
Playground	58
Swings	
The Long Slide	
Roundabout	
Seesaw	
The Given Name	61
Marine Biology	62
Shorelines	63
1 Morning at the Inlet	
2 Jetty	
Museum Piece	65
The Express	66
Genealogy	67
Five Perspectives Including Antarctica	69

from BRUSHING THE DARK (1989)

Out of the Wood	75
The New Arrivals	77
Cover-up	78
Scarface	79
Interlude	80
Visit to Ida Bay	81

Correspondence	84
Acolyte	85
This Place	86
Dusk	87
Beer	88
Interior	89
Telling the Truth	90
Preserves	92
The Rain Snail	94
The Beekeeper's Directory	95
Grapefruit	97
Boom	98
Kelp Harvesters	100
The Mattresses	103
A Harbour-Mistress Recalls Her Wartime Service	104
A Vineyard Quartet	106

from ALBUM OF DOMESTIC EXILES (1996)

Hedgehog	111
Profit and Loss	112
Blotter	114
A Painter in Paradise	116
Willows	117
Typhoon	118
Envoy	120
Haute Locale	121
The Pleasure Seekers	123
Voyage	125
Dénouement	131
from Album of Domestic Exiles	132
LPs	
Sahib	
Mussolini's Umbrella	
Absent Third Party	
Long Distance	136
First Taste	137
The Pedants	139
Shoe Doll	140
Taking My Daughter to the Cave	141
The Conceit of Glass	142
Days of Incompletion	143

from RUSSIAN INK (2001)

Nightfall	147
Caring Accents	148
Stories of My Father	149
1 The Call	
2 Personal Pronouns	
3 Stories	
4 Good Liars	
5 Getting Through	
6 Telling Jokes	
7 Summing Up	
8 Immortality	
Down From Mars	155
The Question at a Station	156
The Skin's Reaches	157
Indian Pacific	158
Waiting Games	162
Walking Along an Estuarine Shore	163
Golconda	164
Red Eye	166
A Shower Medley	168
Snake Words	171
Moths	172
Northerly	176
A Footnote on Torture	178
Belli's Shade	179
A World Without Creatures	182
Pencils	184

from THE ISLANDERS (2002) and THE LIVES AND TIMES OF THE ISLANDERS (2009)

Volcanic	189
Lineage	190
Off the Map	191
Connections	192
Fireworks	194
Old Woman in an Ancestral Mansion	195
A Death	196
A Firework Maker on the Domestic Front	197
Name of the Island	198

Between the Establishment	199
High Views of the Department Head	200
Shooting Season	201
Her Shopping List	203
Wife of a Shooter	204
Elegy for a Dog	205
Out of the Picture	206

from SPEED & OTHER LIBERTIES (2008)

The Sunlight Inland	209
The Morning of the Funeral	213
Poem for the Refugees	214
Nike at the Megaliths	215
Mr Habitat's Home Policy	217
The Oxford English Dictionary	218
Crime Fiction	219
The Lemon Tree at 42° South from 52° North	228
Jasmine in a Temple Garden	229
Exposure	230
Photographs of Shandong Peasant Children	231
Two Ways of Looking at Landscape	232
Attitudes in a Possible Food Museum	233
Heat and Light	234
Voice Theory and Practice	235
Mr Habitat and the Protection Racket	236
Long Wait at Quick Shoe Repairs	237
Saxophone in a Pawnbroker's Window	239
Excursion, Delayed	240
Tasmania	241
The Banana's Republic	242
Abundance	243

from FUEL (2009)

Revisiting Cliffs	247
Marvellous Harbours	249
Mr Habitat's Own Bones	251
Dedication to a Potter Wasp	252
The Household Moth	254
The Marriage Vow	256
Craquelure	257

Heart on a Summer Afternoon	258
Mr Habitat on Terror Etcetera	260
The Heathrow to Melbourne Flight	261
Freddy and the Christening Gift	262
You Are Here	264
Dandelions	266
August	267
Rock Music	269
Interrogative Pressure	271
Change of Address Book	273
Probability Etcetera	275
The Story of a Story	277
Knight	278
The Spider in the Kitchen	279
The Fires	280
Given	282
The Round	284
The Mosquito Satisfaction Wrap	286
Ode to Water	288

from THE BICYCLE THIEF & OTHER POEMS (2013)

Postcard to Hamburg	293
Stone Inclinations	294
Beating the Chinese	296
Speed & Other Liberties	298
Deserter in the Counselling Room	299
Marvel	301
The Other Life	302
Loose at the Zoo	303
In the Villa Gorilla	305
Jack and Yves and Their Many Transports	307
Marine Desire	308
The Bicycle Thief	309

from BAFFLING GRAVITY (2019)

The Tilers	321
Meteorite	322
At The Hotel Splendide	323
Quarry	325

Gravitational Pull	326
To Charleville	327
Expecting the São Jacinto Ferry	329
The Night Journeys	330
Tamarillos	331
Source	332
Mosquito in Amber	334
Mediterranean Time	335
Above the Equator	336
Mood Piece	337
The Queues	338
Machismo	340
Gravity	341
The Suicide Note	342
Lucretian	346
Weight	347
Flexibility	348

NEW POEMS

A Cartographer Dreams	353
Remote Intersections	354
Waspish	355
This Loggerhead Turtle	357
The Yangtze	358
The Watchers	361
Many Sea Urchins	362
Metaphysical	364
American Wonders	365
Territory	367
Acknowledgements	368
Author's Note	368

from LIVES (1980)

LIVES

Henk Ramak's his name: immigrant farmer with a vote —
will drink to his achievement (in local vernacular
he'll boast that conquest) but speaks of disappointment
in Dutch, through dry lips, but rarely, for this popular

man drinks regularly to celebrate the good life. And why not?
His wife, milking, keeps an eye on the track for dust
and a rogue's excuse. "You olt buggar!" and the dairy echoes —
he waves, the Land Rover going past full thrust ...

but he returns, limp with apology, to face the hard life.
There's a conflict: dedication to the good life leaves
small room for the other; he submits, feeds the pigs
dreams of monocled Dutch forefathers, and heaves

the sacks he'd wished on his son. A life simplified
in Australia? The hard life and the good: that strife
might be likened to quarrelsome mistresses
compared to that old seducer he didn't marry, but a life

spiting divorce nevertheless: a plague on Europe!
Thirty years lived with till decent history was struck
by war, shattering family and the orderly dreams —
and still that spectre in his skull will wrestle him in the paddock.

MILKING THREE COWS AT NIGHTFALL

She calls them in, her eyes considering the day's
last labour, she calls them in
her Dutch accent a quiet echo
from the cup of the hills, her life's allotment.

Tonight they come easily: Daisy, Spot, Darky ...
those sad-eyed familiars, swaying
sagged backs towards the dairy
to pay out their milk for a scoop of chaff.

The machinery drones, and she places
the suckers to the hot washed teats,
soon sucking and straining at those loaded udders
so ripe and rude in their full generosity.

And the milk appears to the clinking of bottles
that she carefully fills, times
beyond reckoning has she filled those bottles
watched the outpour of froth make a lick of cream.

Milk bottles placed, and it's suddenly over ...
the cattle released for their ponderous exit;
and solitarily for home she climbs the hill
her last task done, the blood moon rising.

from THE CAUGHT SKY (1982)

THE GEOLOGIST IN A CAVE

When the torchlight's
cone sweeps through darkness
away from the dripping
walls I know I'm adrift
a million uninhabited
years from home
where this persistent
dripping of taps
into pools is the cave
conceding to me
a generous irritation.

Several strata beneath
the veneer of place
(a house, many trees
squared off in a
polished lens) you know
this planet's mostly
uninhabited; and I
go further. A notion
of origins is it
that a rope suspends
me towards?

Whatever is solid
as rocks or facts breeds
echoes as plentiful as those a pebble makes
skipping downwards
into caverns. I collect
samples, like moonrocks,
as if the world
is merely an object
whose diversity holidays
in learned journals –
that slow percolation of facts
seeping through the strata
of libraries.

THE OPTOMETRIST

Inside his house that musty, enclosed smell
as soon as we entered the wide, oak-panelled hall
where a grandfather clock kept unchanging pace
with the comings and goings of regular patients
so that, had a blind man entered, he'd have known
that house by diagnosing its atmosphere –
but I, having been informed on other visits
of my distinguished eye-sight viewed it all
while my mother had her glasses tested.

This was better than school: I always received
unblemished praise for doing nothing
but look around, though the light was bad.
Half-drawn velvet curtains permitted
the wintry light like a slack housekeeper
to polish the abundant mahogany and oak
side-boards, tables, the prim
wicker chairs neatly arranged
in the waiting room. No pot plants

to embroider the enclosing gloom
that must reflect, I remotely thought,
the grim views of this apparently
kindly man who made a living
through others' eyes. Had I been suspicious,
and I wasn't much, this ambivalence might have cast
an early shadow across my view of human nature
causing an unscholarly, cynical leap to think
that he surmised "the world is dark, the blind can see".

His brass was tarnished. I thought of him
inside his office defining the limits
of my mother's vision while I focused on what
I was barely given to see, till, he'd reveal again
I could see it all, down the chart to the smallest
nonsensical, jumbled letters. My mother
would emerge from that waiting room
to hear the news, then I'd race her out into his windy
garden where crocuses flickered like sudden flames.

THE SHORT CUT

Again, I take the track
behind garden fences as a short cut
to a friend's house,
those fences made of packing crates, Cyclone wire
and weathered palings
protecting domesticities they reflect –
patched and battered
and desperately ordered.

When I've gone so far
picking my way
through strewn beer bottle glass
a dog barks,
the lightest sound of an intruder
throttling it to fury.

Though I should expect this
I'm alarmed
when it happens
and quicken my step
for the fear.

The whiff of dogs
lingers along this pathway
amongst wild nasturtiums
whose bright orange flowers remind me
of those exaggerated, pursed lips
painted on circus clowns.

I take this short cut
anticipating my visit –
but always I'm given the feeling
of an imminence
from the uneasy domesticities
that loathe to cower
behind the fences. Within earshot
stale, laconic arguments
erupt unexpectedly, demeaning

as life is for that dog kept half starved
on a short, rattling chain.

GLENLYON

This page is cool light and my shadow's
hovering vague shape from the window behind
defining hazed distances I've come from –
childhood, a city. You could guess my position,
undefined and remote as the nearby pre-settlement hills –
the mind behind the particular mind may be thus:
uncleared, unsettled, mysterious
enough to look into constantly, while passing a window
or else, as now, to turn my back on
and let these passing words settle on the unmapped page.

THROUGH THE PANAMA

The idea of being asleep! –
and sleep is often enough
its own penetrating journey;
but to awaken on the bunk
with a jolt, which was not firm
and abrupt, but sounded
deep down in the ship's hold, echoes
plunging outwards from metal –
or was it the engine? or me dreaming?
Lights off in the cramped cabin and the porthole
glaring with darkness.
To wonder where you are
having scrambled awake
from some dreaming depth
is occasional enough, recollection
easing back slowly towards
that piecemeal "I know". This
time the unhomely recollection
this was our route
through the Panama, and that mute
thundering of resolve and purpose
which found me climbing towards
consciousness and the floodlit deck ...
I leant over the rails
where the yellow paint was sunburnt and flaking off –
exotic smells floated like ripe melons
or bananas gone off in a brand new way
like a teasing introduction
in the still, heavy, intoxicating air.
Who could know what filth
or vegetation made this smell, or care
to be anything other than
a passive onlooker, hanging
over the rails and receiving these
mysteries? Not too dark to see
but I watched with other passengers
what darkness defined

across the suspended water –
the Gatun Lake islands perhaps, packed thickly
with black vegetation, or else shifting
dark shapes tricked by
stillness and moonlight, or
was it that standing there I'd been
absorbed too long on that crowded deck
letting self-consciousness drift
and found those dark islands
shifting, however dreamlike, into the real?

THE SHOE REPAIRER

He is there. He's not fake.
His business survives like his nimble fingers.

He'll knock in a few tacks for nothing.
That's what they say.

He says little.

The past has virtues he maintains.
Diligence. Honesty. Workmanship.

His shop's hard to find;
when he goes he'll take with him a direction.

Notice him, this small wizened man
with metal-rimmed spectacles
humming a tune

over a smelly boot.

Do his customers bear richer images
than words can match?

He keeps on repairing boots, boots, boots.
His jacket stays shabby.

Word gets around, images accumulate.

If you live round here
someone will point him out and say,
That bloke with the dog, he's the shoe repairer!

Then maybe you'll briefly wonder at him.

FANCY DRESS

So the guests meet again
for the first time in drag

on Friday night
after eight at Katy's —

the bloke with a plumed feather
in his hat

that quivers like fire
as he dances

in black tights
with the woman whose sequined dress

flares
like loud music.

Exotic gestures
greet new guests and the film

continues with a dozen poses;
the music's French

enough for eyes to meet
on foreign territory

with no ties —
and it's all for this:

the immediate daring
of restrained desires exposed

with style
across the polished floor.

It's so deliberately outrageous!

All arse
and fair skinned men

pouting strawberry lips
who, prancing

about like antelopes
share a metamorphosis

that invites relief,
or introduces wonder

to old friends
wide-eyed as strangers.

THE FEAR

Butterflies appeared from her childhood garden
without difficulty though memory
cannot identify the first flights
into the terrifying future –
the rose blooms like balloons
still going off somewhere, unfairly.
Was it the unremembered time
in the exclusively dark and still room where
a delicate flutter of air
through flesh froze her for a moment into
the chill frequency of fear?
Memory is blank
but not wiped clean by time
that finds her caught in the garden's
soft scented air, the butterflies blighting the airy
stillness with their codeless messages of fear.

WREN

A wren appears on the branch like an asterisk –

I refer back through
memory to a time of more constant
immersion of self in details –
once this would have been complete experience,
the wren offering itself
for my abandonment in detail,
landing on the fuchsia,
shaking the million purple bells
of my delight.
                    The wren flies off.
I'm left with a footnote of detail
towards an imminent theme.

WESTBROOKE BANKS

Mrs. Irena Pembroke greets
her guests half way down the entrance steps
with a smile like an expensive, cracked dish.
Her hair is bouffant, the touching wind
admires it in a way her husband didn't.
Now the homestead's hers complete
with pigskin visitors' book. The guests
from another state, smile, and sign it
Mr. and Mrs. Wesley Smith; and note the tariff.
She's suspicious of course, nothing's proof
of wealth, least of all a name.
A gong sounds dinner. They enter
the dining room feigning ease
and sit like crows beneath a chandelier.
Her guest, discovering he looks ruffled
beside his wife in a gilded mirror
knows he's never felt so richly ornamental
as amongst this ponderous Victoriana, and expels
some dust from his casual shirt.
Irena Pembroke serves the dinner, placing
beneath her notice each steaming dish
and graciously agrees her ancestors' house is nice;
the guests shield unease at her polished deference.
When coffee's over, the Smiths
inspect the paddocks once hers
where patriarchal boughs of pines
shelter twilit outhouses from colonial weather —
and she, delighted, admires her style
in a convex mirror. She suspects the dark.

CONVICT SETTLEMENT, SALTWATER RIVER

Ponderous sandstone walls,
the odour of dampness, congealed and wintry
inside the cells

so that you can imagine
the convicts alive
in those graves, teased

by chinks of light
and the lively errors
of sound

reminding them that the world
of light was a brute,
marvellously fake.

In this place
there was nowhere further to go
for years;
           then to blink
the colony back –
flat sea, hushed casuarinas
nothing to like.

LITERACY LESSONS

1 A Class of Unemployed Youth

One of the restless lads whose chin
allows sparse wisps of hair tries
to attract the girl with the inviting eye who would,
I figure by her absorption, rather concentrate on another
young suitor who is not here. I'm employed to teach
    communication,
how words used well grasp and deliver meanings.

He pokes her with a ruler. I confront the class
with the hypothesis that literacy abilities,
like earning money, aid survival.
By now, though, there's a general scuffle
under the tables which has me looking for the chief aggressor –
the youth with the thick glasses, or the one who gropes

through a hare-lip. It has me beaten.
So I come down with some
blunt words, hard as sticks on the noisy air.
This, to my relief, impresses
and silence suddenly invades the room
each face gazing directly at me, understanding.

I look at them, these unemployed who hated
school and prefer bullying the dullness of poor streets
with beer, old cars and desperate sex
in secret sheds. Am I serious?
Jeremy, with the gapped teeth, slyly grins
at me and accurately winks to his mate

that the worst's over and it's fair enough
to relax once more. So it goes
and we all know this try out might happen again:
and what of words? Well, so far reverse returns –
I'm wise to their abrupt laconics which, stripped
of correctness, daily penetrate their shared, unlovely prospect.

2 The Improver

It's not so much his knowing sneer across an unshaven face
that discomforts me, or makes me feel
I'm not making inroads into his uncharted mind,
it's the continual shifting on his seat of creaking denims now he's
faced with the knowledge that all he has yet to learn
is exactly what he doesn't
want to know, just now.

How am I to convince him
that an ability to read will get him places?

I develop practical situations
and find work for words
while he sits there hugely,
slickedback hair, broad shouldered
and large hands that convey a powerful message
without a pen. Early twenties.
And would rather be out
shooting rabbits than letting me
set, as he sees it, traps with words.

If I figured he could teach
me plenty he'd agree, I wouldn't doubt –
we'll learn to compromise; he's directed here
to learn skills away from the streets
where he's picked up tricks
to trip up cops, to draw darkness
around him like a blanket which, one dawn
left him exposed in a dewy field
to a troop of police, his cunning
surrounded, and desperate for the right words to come.

from RURAL EPISODES

Duel

As if it could outrun its own shadow
a rat runs hungrily on little pink feet
over and under the log heap
searching with the arrows of its eyes

for a scrap. It'll climb high drainpipes,
take possession of the haystack,
will steal a ripe morsel from beneath
the chickens' pricked eyes, then hide

high in some beams while the black cat stalks.
But this rat fell foul:
in a fury of squeals it bequeathed
its heritage to the wreaths of dust

and emerged from the barn between the teeth
of that tom; a light dripping
of blood followed the carcass
fallen to the bite of this remorseless hunger.

Now the cat is stepping over roofs
still starved and sinewy, while the skin
of the rat lies baked by the sun,
its own mode of payment, a husk.

Blackberries

On the further hillside
clumps of bushes have gathered
monstrously, out in the open,
still disentangled, and it seems they're
prepared and waiting;

the grass is a brown aftermath
of the long, cloudless days we remember
before which they were slashed back
to stalks, and hacked out
with the mattock.
                    Now that refuse
lies like sprung bundles
of tossed, rusty wire
oddly protecting our approaches.

And again we notice
them resurrect, determined and hushed
forever stretching out
over themselves. In this way blackberries
further their interests.

At first the shoots
are green, the leaves opening
like fine wings damp
from a chrysalis, then
experience darkens their tracks
over fences, up tank stands
continuing prickly and hardened
and glistening with the plump
berries of their thrifty progress.

THE RESORT

Dandelions, sunworshippers in
cool climates, populous
and phlegmatic as the Englishmen that lie amongst them
enduring this holiday resort –
those single blooms
across unmown lawns
have tap roots
nourishing in a history
that has known much common ground
but few manorial gardens
so they cleave only
a sufficient space
in the grass

              their compliance
lies in enduring the superior
whims of climate
till age whitens them;
then the puffs
of seed become folklore
picked and blown by children
before the arrival of those unbelieving mowers

HOMAGE TO THE CANAL PEOPLE

Steered straight into this century I see narrowboats
loaded with coal, cheese, vats of vinegar trailing
a hard century behind them along
the polluted Grand Union, yet their cabins are bright
as their paintings of roses and castles
entering Oxford or Chester, a vivid variation
on a theme bleak and slow
as three-miles-an-hour journeys for boatmen
with more rain than sun
working into their faces.
It's pride that brightened them, and acceptance
that heaven's easy chair was far off as the dandies
composing themselves to ignore their progress through towns
like the arrival of gypsies,
cloth caps pulled down against
complacency. So they denied them a privilege –
their cabin doors closed tight
on china, brasswork and lace
fine as webs slung
across the just-after-dawn hedges, yet
those cabins were no larger than a gentleman's pantry.

Long damp days scattering moorhens
from the pounds, then a staircase of locks,
instinctive manoeuvrings through gushes of water,
hard hands straining on ropes
to steady a full seventy foot boat —
I imagine eyes also twisted
like knots between man and wife
till a good pint could loose them,
could knock over incidents like skittles
and with a brutal laugh set them up again;
that's canal pub community
a sharing of feelings, an abandonment
with gossip flying so fast it was prophetic,
the boats outside moored with the children
like all relevant history, in the shadow
of the Swan, or the Bird in Hand.

NORTHWOOD HILLS

There it was, frothy and spit-like,
gobbed onto stems and tendrils
of wild peas occasionally
plentiful in wet fields, if you looked,
the grass so wet it would soak through shoes
quick and cold as a surprise of flu. Nothing
was so varied as a rash of field flowers,
but the mauve pea, its green spirals
of tendrils once picked quickly drooped,
my warm hand clutching moist disappointment.
The gobs of froth were cuckoo-spit,
something to touch, tacky as glue
and recoil fast from over again.
How much I remember. How many
names and accuracies of smell and touch
have mulched into those fields
so deep memory won't resurrect them!
That was ground for establishing
intimacies which have gone
into my mind as roots. I neglect beginnings –
swaying after me, memories that unfurl
sticky as tendrils, touch and infect.

MORNING IN OSLO

At first a puddle's
stillness, a breath

of the Arctic
across the glistening street

will remind you of that wilderness
of ice to the far north

shifting south,
narrowing the keen perspectives

of fishermen
to a few shortening days

of freezing seas
like those pictured

on packets of fish
in a supermarket.

Numbed fingers will recall
the uninhabitable

tundra wastes
as your hands explore

for warmth
in your pockets,

and those sparse populations
whose thoughts

visit here
to be made busy

along the icy
well-trodden streets.

A SENSE OF LOSS

Those evenings when the jukebox
pumped out rock 'n' roll to a bar full

of drinkers at laminex tables
with overflowing ashtrays

– increasingly overflowing
towards closing time

as the pressure
increased

to find in the night's remains
love or oblivion

while the songs
beat out swift reminders

of love lost
or rescued, coins

dropping consistently
into that sympathetic

machine. Until,
it's rumoured around

the bar, the jukebox broke down
and was, with difficulty,

removed for repair
(sorrow's a brute to shift).

WESTMINSTER INCIDENT

Imagine, say, an American tourist
his camera held to a bright eye
at Westminster or Marble Arch
a hectic square of London chosen
by history, recording this fact
of existence, of having been at that
particular fond spot in so-and-so's memory
when out of the blue (or perhaps
more honestly, out of the rude noise)
like an unwanted apparition, say
of the past's power over the present,
this all-too-familiar-face
appears in the lens
and the shock slaps him roundly
on the shoulder, at which time
he jerks the shutter
only to discover much later
(to his horror) not a photo
of the fine architecture
of the past, but sadly
certain pale, disconsolate faces
hurrying, out of focus, towards their future.

MOSS

Unriddle this:
          an old saying
moss hasn't grown on
told in cottages
– roses high as their window sills –
that have crumbled like beliefs
into mounds of weeds

Surviving all weathers
moss clings to walls
where nothing else happens
or else must be scraped
off graves to expose
the dates before
its homage
        Seeing it
can remind me of my grandmother's
pin cushions, that
sewing box emptied
at the busy stalls of
a dozen traceless markets –
proof again moss fattens
along the obscurest tracks

And in overgrown gardens
see it squat on
sandstone walls and steps
– possessive, stealthy –
till owners with shovels strip
those liberties: underneath
dank nests of centipedes, beetles
always a cover-up
             there
where ambition crumbled suddenly
before eventual moss cushioned the fall

MYRTLE FORESTS

Myrtle trees seem to live in fables,
grow lichen beards, are evergreen –

hundreds of years they live
glooming the sunlight gently, in these mountains.

About their roots moss thickens in clumps,
roots set like bones that grasp

the earth we know
we've populated

with pre-historic fictions.
You see trees grope through mists that swirl

about their trunks, lightly
polishing the evergreen leaves

so when sunlight filters
down there's all that leafy gloss and sheen

and a moist tingling of air.
So that is history here –

such buoyant prosperities of light
that surprise and distract

while the owlish and spidery dank
encampments of gloom

throughout the myrtle forest
wait to return.

OLD WOMAN IN APPLE COUNTRY

When dusk approaches
I bring the chair out, and sit –
it's the red vinyl chair
my husband slashed the back of
in a fit, years ago
and I stitched
to make comfortable
after he'd gone. His words
still thunder at me, yet
all the comfort I have was in his hands.
The verandah shades me
from the decreasing light
and the garden has loaded apple trees
he planted, thin whips
of saplings demanding and demanding
those buckets of water.
Occasionally, an apple drops
and I hear his step
on the lawn. But when a car
speeds past, not coating
the trees in dust from the track
I know everything's different –
a hard bitumen laid
across those thoughts. Or else
it's the faces in car windows
reminding me: they are not local.
Noticing me, for a moment
we're each suddenly
foreign somehow, invading repeatedly
each other's difference.
All this happens against
a background of hills
in the cool indifference
of dusk, against which
those apples are hesitant drops
along boughs, the rare light
magnifying their suspense.

TRAILS

1

Memories of this landscape, fossils
under the earth, or a few days back hoofed again
into that sodden mud by cows

making us recall the sea —
those shells, a dense script in hard sediment
that has risen clear of a catastrophe.

2

The house light
after dark flickers

your way back,
secure at its mooring

amongst schools of boulders
surfacing in moonlight.

3

The wind amongst the grass
is the rustling of seas —

this landscape will not forget its past
though it is ancient: hawks

circling over its hillocks
tear at offerings

amongst grasses that pour
over themselves like waves.

from The Flower Industry (1985)

SOUNDWAVES

Selecting a loose vibration from the taut air
and threading it through the wired network
into an infectious signal, the stylish receiver –

translating that which has remained latent,
an invisible vast shimmer of potential
it required aerial genius to unravel,

becoming apparent, now, when
I press a red button and suddenly a full-scale
illusory orchestra, releasing a score,

has assembled beside me, ushering
in a Beethoven symphony, the mind dreaming its composure,
its glitter, many cellos and polished violins

traversing the continent, peak to peak, a relayed signal.
The sound is transmitted only so far:
the weak transistors, in passenger cabins

of liners bucking across the Atlantic
are flawed, ejected from the system
like spent cartridges, until

the unseen peaks of the Indies
are identified, through static, with a jangling
of American music, all ears cocked, intent

– as when the first report was relayed
back from the moon, bounced into kitchens, living rooms –
these immaterial islands all

pace, sound and imagined geographies.
So much is unseen. Here, this far
south, beneath a darkened mountain in Tasmania,

the northern cities' stations, at night, compete
for airspace, fade in and out, like several Mardi Gras,
the radio's occasional brash visitors.

I'll tune in as finely as possible
to the rapid fire of news, the hyperactive
music as if, suddenly, I'm travelling

in a car at high speed where the mind
is a curious receiver, exposed, intent
on that which is always about to be revealed.

FIRES

1 The Observer

When the fire-spotter circling in the light plane
noticed the wide ripple of fire
spreading slowly across the paddock,
he imagined a black sea rising over a blond beach
where each man tamping the fanned flames
feels like Canute.

A row of fenceposts
split from the cleared forest
(a few stands of trees still castled on the ridges)
had burst alive in the heat,
blossoming with flames.

It was as if the cropped hillsides
had been prepared for another harvest;
each spark a seed
the air was filled with, leaping
through barbed wire, across bitumen –
those swift ripenings
on dry ground
in the way films of germination
speed it up.

Through his binoculars
(he said) he could ponder it all
with the detachment
of someone accumulating detail
for posterity –

the hurrying sheep confused as poked maggots

the flywire door, on the tidy abandoned
farmhouse, flapping loose, as if it could not be otherwise.

2 *The Volunteer*

We handled our rakes
(the wind had dropped)
and slashed a break through scrub
a mile long; that was the front,
we had dug in, exposing
earth where even flame
would wilt unlike
the twisting roots, stubborn
against the glinting
blades. We heard it coming,
a gleeful snapping
in the air. Once
in a lifetime
to meet an enemy
(albeit with only
a weekend's training).
But for the haze
it sounded like small animals
scuttling across leaves
and twigs.

Looking back, we were naive.

The wind rose gently,
it cooled us like a sea-breeze
in a calm harbour.
Then I thought of fate, inevitably
– how nothing prepares us for the worst –
as the flames slipped
through the cordon
on that rampage,
tinder snapping like the kids'
cheap fireworks,
and moment by moment
looking for a smokeless
opening I felt exposed
as in a movie, watching
myself at a safe distance,
trapped by curiosity.

THE REASON FOR FIRES

I'm drawn to those who can construct a fire
out of dried wood seasonably discarded by trees

and collected, evidence
arranged, wigwam-shaped, into an argument

for the multiple possibility of flame.
The gathered timber is a construct

that pursues the cold night to an extremity
and so, briefly ordered, is a maker

of what makes us civilised
since the first tribes, naming a place,

gathered there, rubbed word-sounds together
and, with the fizzling of embers, understood

this simile for death, maker of other worlds,
a low technology. This could be nostalgia

in this age of the switch
and the quarterly computerised bill

but this is not so, fires being practical
and available. The hearth-fire though

may produce whimsy, small flames whisking anecdotes
and singeing, perhaps, the divisions of class.

They are also futuristic, there when the oil rig
in the freezing ocean is a windswept monument

besmirched by gulls, having pumped
the guts of the earth. I like a well made fire

in a hearth, an apex, a centrepiece in a room
especially before it is lit,

the kindling balanced neatly in a casual tension
by the maker who, with this preparation

as the first flame leaps, is sure of its risk.

TREMORS

When the investor and the mineralogist
flew over the red humps of mountains
bulldozed, by seismic forces, to the edge

of the continent, the shadow
of the light plane in the glare
was like a fly's shadow circling a rucked carpet

where soon enough there could be
the smash and grab of mine-work
after the careful exploration

of samples, plucked rocks, by delicate instruments.
I have a chunk of raw asbestos,
in my teenage collection of minerals,

from Wittenoom. The silver-grey fibres
of the rock peeled off like strands
of braised steak, harmlessly;

its dust collected in the lungs of workers,
slowly diseased; the stock market was manic.
Another source contains an episode

awaiting birth, unpredictably:
suddenly it is no longer a matter of geology
but appears swollen like a womb

from which will be induced such energy
as will unleash tremors, potentials; it is the future, harnessed,
but a wrong move and the outcome could be lethal.

The mineralogist employs his cool gynaecology
on the sizzling deposit, testing
the cramped swelling of strata, scanning

the data. There may be, in an office,
a financier amongst filing-cabinets and phones
waiting to receive news – achieve immortality –

aching for the climactic phone-call,
his safe stacked like a larder, guarded
and secure from tremors of risk, also a collector.

from STRATEGIES AND REHEARSALS

The Bank Robbers

If, according to plan,
everything went OK
they'd holiday in Surfers Paradise.

Meantime the fantasy
in a dank, rented room that gained
warmth from exotic posters

– tits, bums and phallic palm trees –
would do. The obdurate suburb
marshalled itself around them,

doors clicked shut like handcuffs.
With nothing to do, between nine and five,
they played cards for imaginary fortunes,

a whole pack of escapes,
while prewar movies on TV
gave up their ghosts in black and white.

When one forgot another would remember –
it just takes an acetylene flame
to cure a cold vault of reluctance,

to lead them into a scripted dream.

A Game of Golf

Will today see the arrival of the astonishing shot?
Another whizzing daisycutter deleted that thought

on the fifth, still dew-covered, where magpies
strutted like moving targets, his face inspected by flies.

He saw, again, an arena for perfect geometry
in the still, morning air – those desirable arcs' pure symmetry

after long practice on his pocked lawn, each divot
replaced and tamped, miscalculations that would not re-root.

Imagine he is not an amateur with a blown-out handicap,
uneasy with club and ball and with the trap

of bunkered confidence. He imagines he's not. Good!
Imperative air, generous fairway, he selects his wood.

The Fat Man as Nudist

Is wary of weighing-machines
where kilograms rise like kilojoules.

Notices both the agile quickstep
of thin men along the beachfront

and the watery dance of light
upon which he is moored

close to the margins of the resort
where jokes bob like tossed cans.

He will rise out of the restaurant,
evading punks, settle

into his car-seat
like well-kneaded dough

and drive from shallow comparisons
to the nudist beach, public forum

for a deeper appreciation
of the equality of flesh.

Where the ocean, great leveller,
accommodates buttock and breast

and pride shrivels at the crotch, he'll recline
buoyantly on the bloated sea.

A PROTEST SONG

It's not only we who protest but also they who will not listen,
erecting barricades around themselves, preferring exclusion.

There is no dialogue through walls of police or cyclone fences;
slogans, on makeshift placards, are no substitute for voices.

Slogans are the last resort, complexity reduced
to chants, songs, slow hand-clapping – ourselves abused.

Yet there's a sense of belonging in a crowd that demonstrates,
a common belief that, like sunlight, glows and penetrates –

the issues becoming secondary, unified by feeling.
Conserving forests or pursuing peace, organised marching

or a cool vigil, individuals dissolve in the mass;
though the battles fought within ourselves breed violence,

fears of the unseen: the future. Strange, often the commune
of voices, shedding difference, sing new words to an old tune.

DRIVING THROUGH CONNEMARA

A cold rain sweeps over
the broad valley, tamps faint smoke
of small peat-fires from the remoter houses.

In a past, textbook, epoch
ice camped here; I imagine elegant
Irish elk roaming that forested Siberia.

These barren slopes — all that's left
for us to drive through is the silence of that forest.
Now, look at the roadsides, dark turf

stacked, heaped bricks, sliced
off sodden bogland. History is elsewhere.
Our car is like an insect making a beeline

as if surprised to discover itself exposed.

THE BEHAVIOUR OF PLOVER

Wary, deliberate, plover strut
about the mown grass of common ground, ovals,
in pairs, small flocks

and shift into the air
only after a cacophonous protest
to a passer-by but, unless necessary, not far

and certainly not ruffling their composure
but rather with arrogant dignity
stepping away, thin-legged,

as if that had been their original intention,
as if they are wading in a shallow
looking for something superbly secret

though it is only grass
and you too are surprised, again,
to have discovered them, to be negotiating

their territory. Unlike the owl's
invisibility, in dense foliage, betrayed
by its calling, or starlings that raid

fruit-trees and seed-harvests
in anonymous flocks, plover accept the complexities
of exposure, lay their speckled eggs

in a nest of debris, beside a worn
path, next to a playing field, and defend it
with mannered casualness, each

bird a mirror to the others' pride.
Their behaviour demands explanations:
they expect to be observed,

each vigilant, cool-eyed
behind a yellow mask, wattles; pigeon-sized, olive-grey,
white-breasted, but demonstrably plover, they loiter

with intent to remain,
or ply the air with their discordant
calls to be heard, at a distance,

in houses with closed windows, seizing
attention as would the puzzling
far-off distortions

of a sound-system portending
a deliberate announcement. But
it is a flock loose upon the air,

alarmed, as when unexpectedly
an intruder arrives, gate-crashing
their refinements amongst the stones and grass.

READING FOR PLEASURE

I visit you and you tell me
of the books that you've devoured
in recent weeks, nervously
going for a cigarette, coffee, something
to hold, in need of reassurance.
The walls are lined
with books, and also stacked
like children's blocks: it's
a serious game you play.
This, I suppose, is companionship
since, now your wife's gone,
you live alone – though
not by choice; a restrained way
of living in a world on your own terms.
Though it does not make you happy.
What you digest is analytical –
politics, sociology, semiotics,
which leaves you well disposed
to criticise the revelations
of the daily press, and others.
Your talk is endless
confession, getting it
off your chest in the hope,
perhaps, of retrieving a convert
from the mess. I know it must
be serious being a priest.
Devotion maybe, but I too
have read and could announce
my findings – all this retention
is a result of an infant anal complex.
My friend, you're stuffed with facts!
If you've read the jargon
of those secular priests
we don't discuss it, psychologism
is a bind I guess.
But then, that brimming lilac
you hadn't noticed near your door

is also worldly, a sensual
fact, uncluttered, buoyant, in the evening air.
Read into it, perhaps,
this disclosure: you must continue
to let go, before you start to savour ...

THE FLOWER INDUSTRY

She started from scratch: a few seeds.
She would do this alone, and certainly without men
who, like silhouettes, tramped a visible path

across a paddock to her door. She ignored
those who thought that from society
she'd withdrawn: long dresses, lipstick, shoes.

She spied on them through the jasmine on a trellis
knowing she had not withdrawn but broken through;
from the earth she prodded, flowers blazed symbolically.

She gave away her collection of rock 'n' roll
in favour of the percussion of wind and rain.
Whatever she grew would not be in her womb.

Agapanthus, roses, camellias flourished;
she called the products of her labour
"The Flower Industry" since there wasn't a factory

for twenty miles. The locals waited;
the last of her lovers: mad, they said, inhuman –
with a human fascination. *She's crazy up on that hill!*

She kept the place neat, entirely human
at a true address; but flower-like she'd dream or else
seem intent on something far away or near. Her food was air.

Next thing the lot went up for sale; a risky business.

ELEGY FOR SHOES

These shoes have had it! –
unlaced for the last time, shapeless,
it's weeks since they've been given
encouragement with polish;
they'll join the afterlife of shoes.
Ah, what they have had to put up with!
Innocent bystanders to actions
beyond their control, what
would they believe could they re-
consider the sleazy floors, the immaculate
carpets across which they've strolled,
stoically accepting them scuff by scuff?
So many nights, attendant to
their master, they've waited near the bed
beside her more fashionable, expensive ones
while he, a man of conscience,
dreamed exclusively of the inequalities of shoes.
Each day they would submit
to the brunt of things, toeing
the edge of urinals, racing
pavements unravelling like conveyor-belts –
a life given to harsh determinism
quite beyond question. But also to crafty dance-steps.
Yet always landing squarely, obediently,
the only complaint proffered,
mid-stride, an occasionally
broken lace: utterly matter-of-fact.
Now they're undone completely, exhausted –
the last dog-turd or cigarette crushed
unmemorably during a life of pain.
Stepping beyond the final boundary (disappearing
in the rubbish) as all shoes do
anonymously, their sacrifice
competes with unacknowledged millions
while he, considerate, beyond their knowing,
steps out stiffly in a pair
of shiny new ones which now and now and now,
in early protest, pinch his ankles.

ORIGIN OF THE SPECIES
for Freya

My daughter has captured
wild animals upon sheets
of butchers' paper –

giraffes, apes, possums,
snakes, camels, hippos,
while all afternoon the wind

has shrieked outside like a hyena,
tearing off leaves, kicking
dustbins along the street.

Now her mind is a zoo
that lands an ark
of animals at will;

and they're also free
in the breakfast cereal,
each grinning like a Cheshire cat.

The wind exhausted,
we go outside and discover
a fledgling sparrow on the path.

With "scientific interest"
I see its tiny bellows-
like lungs won't pump

much longer although
for millions of years this effort
has been relayed.

It will not fly
I tell her; she says it will
and later imagines this

on paper. I bury it where
neither tooth and claw nor theory
will interrupt this perfect flight.

PLAYGROUND

Swings

The glistening river the kids notice
tilts back and forth, caught
nevertheless between familiar banks.

They would make the landscape
swing to and fro even faster,
swing it off into space

or make it do a double-flip
and restore itself with the perfect
equipoise of a gymnast.

But they keep stuffing
stubborn air into their mouths,
banging it against their ears

as they swing, push, swing
as if they could also fly above this ground
tricked into suspension by a rigid frame.

The Long Slide

The first downward plunge
was the worst
or best, that imaginary
letting go of something
holding her back
from coming out
of herself like daring
to be reborn for instance
which is a long way
with no escape
once she's going
down all that polish,

falling, falling
insubstantially
to a remarkable thud
on sand. And it's OK.
She climbs trustfully back
up the slope again and again
to make sure she can
let herself go,
thrillingly swoop down
and discover, on her feet again,
she's ready to continue.

Roundabout

When the trees are spinning so rootlessly fast
that they become a dizzying blur, a film

fast-forwarded, and the houses are also whizzing past,
he has corkscrewed to the centre of everything

where colours merge. *Faster! Faster!*
Scooting with his foot simply isn't enough.

Faster! Faster! He leans over the edge.
Later, he will slowly spin to a standstill, focus,

collect his bearings: trees, houses, roads
and, running off, disappear into the periphery of himself.

Seesaw

In this game of weights and measures
it will be proven that he has more kilograms

on his rump. He is grounded: he could shift
and let her plunge down with a shuddering thud.

Oh, the suspense is killing her!
He shifts his bulk nearer the axis

and she floats down so gently, a featherweight,
remains suspended, a counterbalance.

This will go on for a while, shifting
back and forth, the tease, the suspense

of tendencies; trying to give the slip
to the dogged persistence of gravity

in its disguise of grass and daisies.

THE GIVEN NAME

This plant breeds fresh leaves,
green and succulent chains

slightly transparent in the window light.
One segment will ramify endlessly

in thousands of pots
and swift botanical observations.

The refined representation in a book
will be somewhere, out of reach,

on a high, select shelf:
genus and species.

Naming the plant colloquially
we do not think we *know* it less,

coming into our rooms easily, taking cuttings.
A small rite, tame magic

this power of identifying it as
Christmas cactus. Its sudden flowers,

resembling crimson Chinese lanterns,
hang in midwinter until,

frizzled and bleached, their fall
sustains the reverberations of speech.

MARINE BIOLOGY

Equipment in place, electron microscope, notebooks;
no occultist but he believes in formal preparation
and wears a white coat. His fingernails are clean.

Movement without sound through the laboratory window –
trees, busy pathways, a scruffy flowerbed
but more like an ornate partition

between himself and the ocean. This is ritual
and routine; he's keyed-up to observe
but the specimen, like the ocean, is out of focus

and might be, as it was, several fathoms from sight
whilst the ocean and his stomach swayed
wave after wave. What would he come up with?

His hands no longer gripping the ship's rail,
it is the feel of the microscope he loves, instrument
sympathetic to the super-real, eye

into the horrible deep. The lab is calm.
Such controlled conditions! He can pace about
and chatter to himself. Later, later he can translate

his findings into the language of biology –
bleb-like thing that has swum beneath his eye
occupies the immensity of his vision. It will become a word, data.

He will discuss it, over coffee, in the tone
with which he discusses his children's behaviour. Complex
microbe – the privacy of the lab is no escape.

Ah, he sighs, the interconnectedness of things! He'd swear,
sometimes, the floor sways – a lapse of sense –
whilst an oceanic hush pervades his lab, like wholeness.

SHORELINES

1 Morning at the Inlet

Thin mist over Bruny Island
has lifted; a dozen cars
line up obediently for the ferry.

There will be business as usual
(light polishes the store window
the young woman is washing)

while a man balanced in his rowing boat
shoves it off the narrow beach
with an oar. Soon,

anchor dropped, his boat rocks
gently in the lambent bay.
It is only when the wake

of the green ferry bucks
his boat that he's divided
from his dream

and glances up, inspects his bait.
Low hills around the inlet are the outlines
of his next recollection.

The morning light has dissolved
the scattered boulders
on the beach; the distant

repetition of a woman calling
is substantial, urgent. But now
famished gulls that trailed

the ferry swoop
and falter above his boat,
hurling their cries

of anxiety, rending
the watery silence, as from the ferry
the disembodied, thin whine

of a transistor radio is heard
while the boat churns
down a corridor of light.

2 Jetty

Nine a.m. An empty desk in the raucous classroom;
on the jetty a small boy studies flathead in a plastic bucket.

A fishing boat, festooned with gulls, ties up at noon;
the skipper, scratching his bristles, thinks of women.

Midweek, little happening, a bicycle abandoned;
three years since the young man drowned.

On the headland a woman, remembering, looks across;
the jetty an insect's feeler testing the emerald water.

And now the tide, utterly detached, repeating an experiment
balances and weighs the jetty's reflections.

MUSEUM PIECE

There's a huge slab of creamy sandstone
lifted, with ropes and tackle, from a valley

and now displayed in the museum's
constant, fluorescent light;

the evenly spaced tracks across it,
no larger than a cow's, are beelining towards extinction.

In these cool Victorian rooms is the established silence
of a building steady on its foundations;

a reminder this is a stable continent
upon which the city is settled –

a suddenly conjured map of directions.
Where schoolchildren horseplay,

recreations of prehistoric beasts
tower; remote structures scoured

of function. It's like looking at X-rays.
Now, wandering amongst glass cases of fossils,

if I consider what we will spare
for such curious bystanders as might

wander into some futuristic lunchbreak
we're annulled! The heavy entrance door gravely

opens and closes – sounds of traffic and crowds
breed and as suddenly evaporate.

THE EXPRESS

The bus travels at an inevitable pace
south along the corridor where towns are assembled
like old furniture: scant, ramshackle
gestures of settlement.

The few clothes in my bag
which earlier draped over the iron bed-end
are disordered, illustrate a leavetaking.
In my mind I reconstruct time

withheld in rooms before this journey –
the early sunlight was never so obliterated
by drawn red curtains while we turned
to wake; but now it's your face

that halts me against the fleeting landscape –
humps and tussocks, dumped machinery in parched fields
that hesitate and disappear. Now over such distances
you remain entirely, untouchable, perfected.

GENEALOGY

He considers his parents' faces
and sees traces of his own fast
disappearing in slackening flesh –

brown eyes, squared chin, aquiline nose.
The sum of generations remains particularly
in the power of a carried name to identify the landscape

of a face: so who is he? where have his genes come from?
Acquisitive, he has the collected details to hand
and admires his science. The recent

photographs, for instance, of his grandparents
long dead – all is relative;
they seem barely out of reach, after the war,

and stand beneath an abundant plum tree
whose fruit he's eaten. Perhaps
it's still prolific or, like them, has been lopped

whereby, he concludes, that common and proper
names are twinned. The plum flowered regularly
between dates on the certificates

of birth and death he studies.
How they travelled! It seems their small allotment
was like a ship that picked them up

and cast them off. He has the tickets.
Less exacting evidence for their parents
and their parents' parents

with names like George and Alfred, Emily and Victoria,
and some dates. For these
he thumbed through parish registers

and inspected graves. Damp stains
on paper, gravestones worn smooth or cracked,
he imagines ancestors far away, further back, alive

in their damp cottages: the smell of beds
in candlelight, wind against the thatch.
What was their trade? He consults his notes.

Through him they'll speak their names again
as if he's a medium; but evidence thins and thins
like faded ink. An uncertain wilderness

begins, unreachable, where people lived.
The past is another frontier: he dreams at night
of unidentified folk appearing to mouth their names.

FIVE PERSPECTIVES INCLUDING ANTARCTICA

1

It is there, curious, inhospitable
as outer space, graveyard
for the hero-explorers; and some
who returned were compelled to go back

to the snow, great emptiness,
to peer out through the ice
plastered across their faces.
We read about it in books.

Impossible! Impossible!
Yet if extremities are close,
reading about them gives them a place
other than here.

2

A man, in a heavy overcoat,
steps out into a London street:
hearing the easy swish of buggies
he thinks of ponies and sledges.

It is 1910; his name
will be synonymous with Antarctica
when his beloved empire
has melted to a few outposts

and ideas about origins have gone
beyond the blasted, frozen frontier
where emperor penguins guard their eggs.
In extreme innocence he gets lost in the crowd.

3

The Antarctica display
in the Tasmanian museum:
photos of scooped and sculpted ice

in sunlight, penguins
in full dress, fat seals
on their floating waterbeds of ice

invent a benign wilderness.
I think of explorers in extremis
who faced no more

or less than anyone else
in a seemingly comfortable house.
I think of Antarctica as metaphor.

4

If the tilt of the globe altered
(an inconspicuous adjustment in space –
a lightly breeze-blown egg)

and the icecap shifted
off its pedestal of rock
and slipped into the sea

with a gigantic, scrupulously slow heave,
it would create shock waves through water
similar to those you have seen when a pebble

is dropped into a pond and, in nature,
equally significant. But imagine those glinting fish
you disturbed swimming about the house!

5

When the balmy tropics,
for some, are winter dreams
where vines twist upwards before their eyes
in exhilaration at the heat,

I dream of the south, here,
where snow is already a companion
to the nearest mountain,
an intimation of proximity.

Antarctica: under two thousand miles south –
all sea! The wind has memorised
the cold as shared fossils memorise
the drift of continents.

Under the ripped and crevassed
Antarctic ice huge forests
have collapsed as strata; we seize
a rest from past and future

amongst our dreaming trees.

from Brushing the Dark (1989)

OUT OF THE WOOD

If x-rays are nearsighted
our craftsmen have looked into wood
like visionaries; whose hands

have been sympathetic
as healers', fingertips touched
what is not yet visible,

as if the vibrations
of the thunderously toppled trees
are stored there for release;

and so compelling is this energy
they have to refine and polish their wares
like love or scrap them completely.

Consider the Huon pine bowls and vases –
one man has entered a two-thousand-year-old
tunnel of cellulose with sharp tools

and imagined them, he jokes,
to be as perfectly preserved
as sacred artefacts in an Egyptian tomb;

a treasure-house jammed
with nameable goods
and clearly not visible

in the panel of light
the superfast chainsaw revealed
when the huge tree unbalanced from its hinge.

Now I, loving their drive
for discovery and embracing it
expectantly, see our jostling trees

with a curiously deepened pleasure
in the way the conductor's baton-maker might have
before I saw him playfully

raise his polished batons,
in the absence of an orchestra, as if he heard
startling music alight from the wood.

THE NEW ARRIVALS

The tick tick of a sprinkler
spitting territorial water,
and the comfort of hydrangeas ...

In the bureau a nook for their passport.
She idly reads "allow the bearer
to pass freely" and strokes it

like a talisman, a needle's itch
still plaguing her arm,
a pale scar stamped there.

These days spent in a slipstream
of songs from home, setting
furniture, crockery in their places

here; the children swiftly at school –
and he'll leave his mark:
the company car spurts gravel

sharply at eight and is gone.
A question hovers like a mosquito
whining in the dark – how long

will it take to truly arrive?
Now she has set her children's shoes
at the door opened to the sky

and gums surrounding the lawn:
light simmers there amongst shifting leaves,
snake and spider coolly shadow the roses.

COVER-UP

It occurred to me that since our house was built in the 1870s
it must be made of convict bricks; now, scouring a wall, it
   occurs to me again
that behind plaster and paint there are convict bricks,
some with a sweaty thumbprint signature, convict colophons,
baked into orange clay and as permanent as those other
   inscriptions,
the welts of the lash that encouraged these walls piecemeal out
   of the ground;
and it occurs to me that each brick forms part of an unwritten
   history blasted
by a hell-fire that could bake a million bricks: a few thousand here
with solid life-everlasting behind plaster and paint.
I could expose and study them, they are those convicts' only
   gravestones
as befits the anonymity of those wearers of dun-coloured
   uniforms
but I'll keep them sealed off, not only for practical purposes
but also from better society. I think of the brogue of the Irish
and the witty cockney tale-spinners exiled in Tasmania
behind the hugely substantial indifference of distance;
and I am walled in, a keen listener amongst the dumb bricks,
   with windows
wide-open to admit the fresh breeze, the sail-raising westerlies.

SCARFACE

In the obedient emulsion
of his skin the slash
of a wild knife, its lightning,

down the alley that was damp
with piss, sherry
and cleansing drizzle;

the office-blocks stood as tall
and implacable as opponents
in dark masks: a few late

lights on to let you know
they meant business. Whoever
has seen the popping of a flash-bulb

will know the swiftness of harsh retribution
and avert sly eyes
from the image in his flesh,

the vertical grin stitched
in his cheek. Scarface,
petty swindler, rogue,

his police-file excessively thick
as a novel with collaborating
authors' alternative endings –

and should all possibility finally be handcuffed,
the official inks of poised biros
must slowly congeal like blood.

INTERLUDE

As a nurse unfurls a white sheet
snow settles over the town: only
the very old remember.

The moraine of memory holds fast;
cold has entered frail bones.
Will the lemon trees survive it?

Our windows have thinned and look!
snow is falling again,
erasing my footsteps – deep

forgetfulness everywhere, surprise
innocence of parkland and wharf.
Complete freeze: apple and pear

will be a little crisper, holders
of the cold ocean
of air from the south; this

polar rehearsal on ponds rivets
ice exactly, baffies
moorhen and duck;

and swerving parrots assume
the snowflakes are moths, a plague
riddling the air –

the whole town shares a hunger for metaphor!
A blanket, a quilt ...
Quick, we say, humanise this event.

The roads, schools, ovals are a silent
dimension of white for a day – a week?
Snowmen, wall-eyed, are obsessed with the present.

VISIT TO IDA BAY

Wheezing steam, the green engine
becomes a cocky pioneer
that blows its top as we jerk

from the station, which is sheds,
a gravel clearing in a brackish
flatland where weatherboard houses

have lurched sideways and stalled.
At ease, you could correct your watch
by letting it stop; the fern fossils

suspended beneath bog
record this afternoon as an instant
exposed to the rattle of carriages

and to coalsmoke that smells
of elsewhere's central stations
amidst the salve of eucalyptus.

This trip's for our children
whose latitude this is, who'll recall
the whistle as we speed

past the marble gravestones
of timbercutters —Tylers'
three white exclamations

amongst scrub whose species
none can name. Yet they're alert
to the button-grass with its extra-

terrestrial antennae
and to the white bonnets of irises —
a local gathering the sea-breeze flurries.

This forest's an esplanade
if this train's an express!
Irredeemably unromantic are the ruins

of an early settler's cottage –
a eucalypt, impatient
for its station in the sky,

has tossed walls aside;
and in the shallow bay
his wharf that will no longer

accommodate cargo –
those black officials, the cormorants
have sequestered it. Did that settler

receive this message?
Brilliant water continues
its Morse code through trees.

His view perhaps thus:
as singular as this narrow gauge
that curves as we sway

past black swans posing
a question, or a burst
of cockatoos whose gutturals

grasp the air, the roots
of this forest where a fur-swaddled
race camped beneath bark –

humped among scrub
each midden is their testimony,
deep strata, riddled

with the bleached sockets of shells.
Now the steam shrouding us
reflects the impatience of pistons

like children – where are we?
When will we be delivered?
Lurch, halt and wheeze.

This train's become an act for a boozy
picnic's standing ovation while
the barefoot children slip away to the sea.

CORRESPONDENCE

If they could hear the machinelike decisiveness of hoofs
in the undulating olive grove they could hear the future echoing
before news had become news, these wizened slaves
lifting their heads, heavy with distances, to see
a messenger with fast-forwarding thoughts that are of teeming
    Rome,
little puffs of dust in his wake settling like gossip, the rhythm
of an emperor's heartbeat just heard in the bleached provinces.

He will arrive here, that messenger's distant descendant, the
    postman
without news of acres soaked in blood or an excuse for execution
to crimson a cool toga. Will it be bills, a small cheque,
a letter fresh from the swift circuits of a sorting-room's
international effusiveness? In provincial outreaches blood
may be expended slowly; it's common to banquet on
    endurance, mindful
of the hawk that plummets, clutches a mouse, and swallows it
    whole.

ACOLYTE

In a shop whose walls have been abolished by polished mirrors
which multiply faces that have leapt from glossy magazines

and where a potted palm, with the shine of an ornament,
is a cool investment in style, the hair-stylist preens himself

and minces between his clients, flourishing a blow-drier
and thin scissors. His assistants, the wind, rain and sun

usher the women in, or it's the air-conditioning
like a husband's gentle, controlled indifference

or panic that swells like a wrinkled hag in the mirror
of a mahogany dresser, a clock ticking, ticking

that leads them to his touch which tingles like sequins;
and he's the distant acolyte of a Parisian

fashion hierophant, who conjures style like cocktails,
who brushes away seasons like dyed hair

and seduces change, to this cumulus look
which, crossing the world, halts in the mirrors

of Jeremy's Hair Fashions. Now it's spring.
Cherry trees toss their confetti, wattle foam and fizz in the hills,

and Jeremy will ravish his ladies
with dyes and wigs and curls.

THIS PLACE

A match flares, it's a jogging toy-flame.
Candlelight and moonshine will guide us
but the mood's not romantic when the power's off,
then on, or flickers like a spluttering firework
while darkness attempts to connect,
while the huge turbines keep spinning,
while water rushes headlong to spin them
as it breaks free of the dams held by mountains like overseers;
and the galaxy lights of the town, the molten bar-heaters
are like brilliant wishes the water releases
which is also our technical conjuring at work
in the darkness that overshadows it.
Reconnect us at once! Some light-droplets
we see in the sky may just be the after-spray of extinctions
and that's the end of the matter;
as it was also for the water-globules
that could hiss, spit and expire on our red-hot
stove-top, leaving a black patina.

DUSK

When the telephone rings persistently like an alarmclock
it can be dealt with. Rush to baffle it! Silence brims again
    everywhere
after the shrill gurgling of the one sound that has syphoned it.

Telephone-wires here have another use: the starlings' roost.
I hear them at dusk gathering over the house, the excited
    twittering
as if so many crossed wires cannot contain the hot news.

This is their restless Kings Cross, rush-hour manic,
or it's like a boiling demonstration – no, dizzy fans gathered
at a pop concert: such sizzling vibrancy

setting off bird-alarms. Bring out the hoses to extinguish them!
Rain is their element, they'd ruffle their feathers'
oily iridescence in the spray that might reach

and it would seem a thousand wings must fan and combust them
as cleanly as anthracite. I stand about, watching expectantly.
A high bellows-like wind puffs and buffets the clouds for a late
    sun to ignite.

BEER

Torpedoes look as harmless as these do on the racks;
my friend who makes beer explains that one brown bottle, at
 his place,
has exploded. We lift the bottles from the fridge as if they
 were meringues.

The valley hop-fields, staked as if for giant beans,
are picturesque: tourists photograph them, and the oast houses
with their brittle weatherboards, that stand firm as early prosaic
 churches.

Sober plantations (in straight rows!) and the cameras memorise
 them –
river-flats, hills, literal perspectives. I remember them also
but in seeing them heard the quiet detonations of the fruit-
 clusters

forecast, but forestalled in the picking. Instead
they travel out of sight, as seeds might, to reappear picked
and riotously transformed at a party. The barley-field also.

My friend has the chemistry, a potent recipe.
I've watched the brewing, the horrible slow frothing, the ceaseless
fermenting bubble and fizz; and have heard his buoyant
 admonitions,

the crude incantations. It's fertility that's at stake.
When I lift the tops the force of the beer also lifts them
and imitates, with relief, a fart or a burp. Let's celebrate!

The beer's dark; and it will speak through us while through our
 blood
streams this memory-photographed concoction that will
 transform and dump us,
as if splayed in a field, through the rough-tillage of headache
 refocusing.

INTERIOR

See those poppies rise from the glass vase
like delicate charmed snakes, the buds questing, alert.
Was it avarice or praise that cut them cleanly from the garden?

Now, swelling in unison, they burst furry sheaths,
which litter the soft carpet. Look!
Reds, oranges, whites – stamens thick with gold pollen.

Or look at them this way: they're simply at the mercy
of process like stars speeding through space
towards extinction, good-for-nothing fertility on this shelf.

TELLING THE TRUTH

Matron leaned towards me
if I conjured the monkey,
her dress endlessly white
in the dining-hall's gloom.

Gentle administrant
of bandages and Dettol
she was the lipsticked madonna
of dormitories orderly

as stern barracks or wards.
Our house seemed like a zoo.
Cats, newts, a canary –
punctilious blue-tits

flitted like coal flames
through the nesting-box hole,
worms twisting in their beaks,
doing loops, S's and O's;

and in the garage mice slummed
in a Hong Kong of stacked cages.
So why not a monkey? Matron
listened, matron's smile was the light

towards which exotic plants stretch
or where monkeys grip speed
through evergreen trees. Call
him Albert, get him dressed

in red dungarees, a peaked cap
and recall his adventures
(he has the run of the house)
should she ask, should she ask.

Matron smiled, matron listened
as she did to playground distress.
I might wonder now how such a monkey
escaped, and if she guessed

that my thoughts made him real, an imp
visiting lunch. Did she starve him
of light? Or was it boys whose eyes
trapped the meaning of blush?

PRESERVES

Too soft and they'll drop! Summer swelled with daylight
and warmth till plums were its purple or yellow reflections
and, loose as worked buttons in our trees,

set for bottling. Mother's pronouncement stopped clocks
as she arranged the hoard amidst curtains of webs
on the top pantry shelf. Climb up and look.

I'd have liked birds' embryos too, or adders
suspended in formalin, newts, shrews, baby otters
as if glass only withheld them from the tocking pulse

that cracked blue-tits' eggs in the catproof birdbox
or paced field-mice sprinting from the garden shed.
Like swift verdigris the blemishes settling on a stale loaf of Hovis

that smelled of musty decay in the enamel bin –
an airless attic smell fit for storing
discarded goods in: up there were deep trunks of clothes

that had been shed like skins. You'd think of bones, ghosts
that fancied they suited them, a stirring half-heard like bats,
moths' wings brushing the dark. But our kitchen

was pip-riddled preserves and light angling wetly through
    cube-ice
or the orange spots of a plaice like frosted globes
glowing on the sea-floor of the fridge;

or, in other kitchens, there was cheese
to warp time – in other kitchens that trapped
acrid taste, those smooth moulds flesh-pale and clammy.

A word, nevertheless, to make us smile and blush.
Say cheese! It's spring and we're beneath the hum of
   blossoming trees
and there's father with his camera making spools of us

or retelling his gothic microbiological joke
that made cheese seem like rot, a seething culture
of organisms that could creep slowly, oh slowly

off platter or plate. I'd watch, if we ate out.
Didn't other folks guess? Stilton, Gruyere, Danish Blue ...
On those long evenings the grown-ups seemed cool, pale, aloof.

THE RAIN SNAIL

There is a puzzle here. Why is it
that this snail with all its belongings on its back
like a weatherproof rucksack has travelled so far distant
from its rock-bound, well-settled, water-happy relatives,
the oyster and scallop, to cruise the bird-riddled
rarely damp territory my back door opens on to?

A thousand miles away, over the Southern Ocean,
there will be clouds rushing this way like an armada of
    billowing sails;
in the sea-shallows the molluscs are feeding
or, fed on, will receive
the sudden twist of a knife;
and here is a snail excreting its river-bed mucus,
onto dry concrete, which it glides across.

It must be ravenous! The first to arrive at the crisp, dainty
    lettuces
it leaves a trail not unlike an excess of saliva;
I follow its muscular, deliberate progress with steady interest.
Its jaws ripping at leaves must, in the snail-world,
reverberate like the sound of crumpling metal. Suddenly,
I think I hear them but discover it's a bird-sucked shell crushed
    by my boot.

Petit escargot! Your species are provided with their own
    gardens in France.
There are snail-crowds also clustered under my log-pile, a
    damp refuge.
Those rubbery antennae they'll peruse the atmosphere with
are retracted till tomorrow or the next day
when the rains come like a continuous spray from a river or sea;
and as if ancestral memory, long brooded about, reminds them
they'll slide out into the wet and follow this snail that predicts it.

THE BEEKEEPER'S DIRECTORY

1

While bees scale the sun-heated front walls of the hives
that are arranged like a terrace, weatherboard and white, on the hillside
and other bees cruise above (it's rush hour at a European airport)
or land on the sills of hives with their harvest of pollen
as if particles of light have never been such a burden to drag forward
or nectar, which will be the packed and condensed memory of summer,
such a ponderous gluttony; while the beekeeper, thinking this,
snaps a switch of broom to flay, clear of his face, the flies
whose continuous buzzing hoops and girdles the valley,
its pardalotes, its butterfly irises, with the monotony of sweat-shop machines;
while a brown hawk flutters on the palpable air;
while a polished skink basks on a flat rock –
his new neighbour assembles a bee-hive, looks skyward
to where the bees are, and gazing vaguely about for advice discovers
the beekeeper's oblivious face, honey-coloured in sunlight.

2

The bees give him authority. Hungary exiled him,
which is where he'd track his father, in leather boots, trekking to his hives
which was also a bee-trail from their garden: on his mother's thick bread
the sweet and sticky garden, the essence of flower-heads, he spooned it.

He thinks of empty honey-pots, he thinks of Europe, licking
   the rims
as if licking the undulating distances where the bees flew to the
   villages.
In each pot the thick, golden sunlight, the deepening afternoons.
Drip the honey through the window-light: he says, there, look! –

at first it swells heavily at the edge of the spoon
and then is like molten amber glass flowing continuously from
   a height
with such pure consistency to pool smoothly on bread
(or for the fun of it!), reflecting neither exile nor boundaries.

3

He claims the bees describe their directing dance within the hives
like swirling ice-skaters, for whom he's the thrilled audience, and
knows by this which eucalyptus trees flower, then goes
   there breathlessly

and expects bees. He has also seen his neighbour's bees
and his neighbour's blundering, since for him a hive is just a
   honey-factory
that goes slow, goes on strike, swarms from the entrance, migrates.

Since he bee-worships he can fancy himself as a priest
whom his neighbour must approach deferentially to extract the
   honeycomb secrets;
he'll say workers are shirkers with a tired queen, and smile keenly.

That's one factor. He says the bee-hives are restless
   communication
circuits, alive with messages, and listens closely to the deep
   hum of old Europe
interpreting the shining eucalyptus forest, refining it;

and he boasts its energy flows into his blood that's nourished
   by good honey.

GRAPEFRUIT

The lights are full on in the grapefruit tree, a hundred
yellow lights wired-up and dangling from spindly branches –
no wonder I pull the blind down late at night,

all that energy stored in plump fruit during the hot summer!
I witnessed this one morning while threading
a fuse that had blown, brilliant electricity

banished from the house cool as pale dusk,
the light-globes hanging like ghost-fruit
for the efficient switches to resurrect;

and I thought of the benefits it's said
that come from gorging citrus quickly after it's picked,
that charged-up incandescent freshness;

and I thought of the stallholders touting it in the market-place,
those barrow-loads swollen with juice, its liquid voltage
sold in the heat of volatile early-morning bargaining …

A pip I pressed once into damp soil was a code
for bountiful fruit, a message, and I transmitted good wishes
from my fingers. It received me and broadcast its leaves.

BOOM

Under the glittering ocean,
under buckled strata, all
that can be known of a great rainforest

is a trapped lake of oil
in a mist of gases. For the
earth will harbour its secrets

of the frisky spoor of ferns
that delivered their fronds delicately
into sunlight

and of massive trees, pure force
fattening their boles that stood
rooted in motion, whooshed

stealthily skywards, igniting
leaves and exhausting them.
This lake is the forest's silent underworld,

a steamy bird-call tropic collapsed
and condensed, the Carboniferous
squeezed to an essence

of speed which,
if we could see it,
is happening everywhere.

Drill for it!
the Board of Directors said,
and the forest reasserted its pace,

became progress in a headline
OIL HOPES SEND SHARES ROCKETING
and the sharemarket was recharged

or was it rumour merely
that set phones ringing like alarms,
rendered the shares flammable,

made brokers discard their jackets,
each digit underwritten
by the possible ghost

of a huge forest;
and there was only a slick
swaying on the sea at first,

evidence of an unstopped genie,
its powers vast
and volatile –

that would vex the atmosphere
with its carbons from cars
as plentiful as wishes.

KELP HARVESTERS
(King Island)

The men who harvest the bull kelp
hold licences to do so: they are the initiates,
the powers are working for them even while they sleep
inside flimsy houses moored in the wind
that, by daybreak, will have dredged kelp like dye
streaming through waves, the ocean's
hydraulics set in motion somewhere off
the African coast – a hurricane through the swirling kelp forest.

Scavengers, they might be from early shipwrecks,
emerging from wind and rain in their dungarees
or stripped off, the island (a passing eyeful from the air)
becalmed in sunlight for, as they say, if you don't like the
        weather here,
wait five minutes: harvesting one day, the next
plunging into cold emerald water to where encrusted wrecks
are alive with abalone and crayfish, boats anchored
clear of the last gusts of wind that might have carried
        beseeching voices

way beyond the lighthouses that attracted brigs, schooners
to the island like moths, white, huge-winged and flying east –
those lighthouses they thought signalled coasts
to the north and south: surprise island, remainder-land, battered
plateau of a subaqueous range hoarding its threat
in the night and ready to strike, waves lashing
the coast as a whip flays a bowed back; and a ship's
charts and compasses were crude charms to outsmart the dark.

Well, they left their names on the map, identities
marking the island's extremities: Whistler, Martha Lavinia,
        Cateraqui –
many vowels for the wind sifting the sands of the unmarked
        graves
of the drowned washed up and dumped on the beaches, dressed
in tresses of kelp. Stand there and look.
The ocean, richly possessed, breaks on the rocks to break again

and in the air there's the complexity of oyster-catchers and
    gulls, pheasant
streak inland also perfectly at home with the singular tones

of the sea: they are variations on the theme of survival.
The ruffled pages of the waves have travelled a long way with
    their science
but, turned so fast, only the molecules of the dead can
    comprehend them
as they swirl through their origins at these shifting littorals.
They have become other, having passed through
and beyond the purgatorial stink of kelp that's there, now, but
    lying fresh
on the sand, that glistening algae, ripely primaeval,
ready to be hauled, in a frenzy of tractors, across the huge dunes.

Hunting and gathering on the island (mutton-bird for supper!):
a jet overhead unzips modernity; and they, whose wives,
if not partners in the harvest, are moored in houses and may
    not converse
for hours, days, except with the wind thinning its vowels
on the telephone wires and in the familiar instrument of
    stacked bottles,
they, the harvesters, dragging kelp before rot drags it back,
are parties to a transformation like a keening
of language, a common industrious magic.

The rattling speech of the drying kelp on its racks
at the factory is prosaic: it speaks of alginates, cash-flows;
death, that has demanded the emptying of so many bottles
at the top of its slipway, is a comatose ocean, mapless, and no
    place
for exports is the message of the drowned in the whispers of
    wavelets;
the changes continue to begin: mysterious? bizarre? Not here,
    not now,
not for the harvesters circumventing the island where
the present changes gear on roads through alterations of
    weather.

Just for now great change, discovery or loss, will happen elsewhere
and it must, hugely, as once this island intervened in the night –
but not now, in this calm, while the bagged granules of kelp
are swung into the ship, rudiments for recipes of these:
ice-creams, dressings, detergents, cosmetics, glazes and paints ...
Who, in an emporium, would be thinking storms assist their
 formation?
On such a day, with its breezes, the harvesters will fish off
 fresh beaches,
and their wives will be washing the clothes that reek of process.

THE MATTRESSES

Because speech mends the frayed
past invisibly, I'm sheltering
in a laminex cafe

imagining mattresses surfing
fatly through waves from the wrecks,
stuffed to capacity, seed-rich –

that harboured warmth like nests,
sleepers tossed into the sea
like recklings, King Island's reefs

swimming beneath them
on a night of big winds that now discover
a street. Ironic bounty

this tale that recalls the mother
country's mementos being dumped
to burst on white beaches

for those sowers of freshly
stripped paddocks, the breezes,
and mingling rains from the west.

Lush pasture now, cow-beds.
Such stories become homely
as companionable pillows –

and this one, overheard,
a zesty ingredient as I spoon
this smooth and delectable cream.

A HARBOUR-MISTRESS RECALLS HER WARTIME SERVICE

The steady throb of a motor round the headland
and my ears were tuned to the night's stethoscope –
front door ajar, while the kettle steamed slowly
above a fire that could flicker till dawn; and so I picked
a way through trees that paused in the dark,
my leathers creaking as I strode to the beach.
Just then I'd probed the reefs better than any other.
There was my boat snug in its cove, the moon
a gash of solid light in the water pooled
between the seats, or it was a pale sea-furrow
bright enough to guide boats home. Otherwise
it could be push and shove as if restraint
was the island's purpose, a mountainous
No to all my efforts while a westerly
thuggishly seized the she-oaks on the ridge:
this island underestimates its children.
For always the boat came free as if gravity
turned a blind eye to me, surprised to find
such stubborn purpose dressed in colourful skirts.
Say, if you will, those years made a man of me
for sure enough the fishermen swore
what they liked, out of earshot, into the wind
and it seemed I'd beelined into the tussle
of their conversation, my pilot-light flirting
with their innocence; and so what if I took
the odd one home for more than toast and tea?
Fiercer than the wind was the jealousy
of Bass Strait women whose powdered faces
missed an opportunity in this no-man's-land
of sky and sea: their men straggled back
in ones and twos to place crushed slouch hats
on prominent hooks, and the comfortable bitches,
clinging to their shirts like bats, pitched horrid gossip.
Siren? Slut? I had to look that first name up.
Then eyes appeared to shine in the tea-tree thickets
around my block, and feet snapped tinder:

not wallabies but those of kids who'd never know
this port was strictly run, the log books kept
as orderly as I kept my house. To prove it, later,
why did I have to keep sweeping and sweeping
until finally I had to count and collect
yellowing leaves direct from the trees?
But here's a window now with a treeless view,
compliments of what I call the Hotel Imperial
where from bed to bed go nurses with their secrets
and the sea-wind visits with its crews of voices.

A VINEYARD QUARTET

The sombre vineyard in winter, all antlered;
a perfect grid of monoculture, rulered over slopes;
these long contours of computer estimates, sober figurings;
boneyard of dreams, I like mine as well-fleshed
as the images a plump wine creates from its flavour and bouquet
long after the curious tourist has revealed a cluster of grapes
amongst leaves in folds like a conjurer's cloth patterned with
    figures.

*

When I met the great-grandson of a winemaker
he was the double of his whiskered ancestor, a recent Noah,
who gazed steadily from an oval photograph
in the tasting room, a stern bequeather of grapes,
their hectic sugars and randy yeasts
swarming through vats with a corpuscular energy –
a family bank where the interest compounds daily,
disciplined alchemy attracting customers in planeloads
who need a drink to comprehend it;
and the great-grandfather was buried nearby
where a vine stretches and twists like lineage ...
his stiff collar and tailored waistcoat abandoned,
this breeder still pursues his vocation, fruiting
bountifully, the great-grandson said, passing a glass,
a toast to the whiskered image, piquant ghost in the alcohol.

*

Born near the vineyard,
her name is the vineyard's,
married at the vineyard
in a white dress, her lipstick
claret-coloured. Luxuriant serenity!
Glasses raised for the toast, the massed guests
appraise her cool beauty
and the groom, well-heeled,

is well-pleased till an unexpected guest,
a Mr Dionysus, arrives unannounced,
steps like an apparition
through a laden vine; and he is also well-hung
in his briefs though a little drunk
and as he approaches her nipples ripen.
No, he's that seasonal picker
from Mildura who she's watched
while he's watched her on the verandah
or riding by, high in her own estimate,
on a roan mare. This is her fear
when she sees him lift his glare,
clear of the bottle he's slaked
his thirst from, and grin.

*

Go into the cool cellar,
step down out of the light
busy as fingers on the vines
at once polishing and rubbing out;
go down into the tomb-darkness
and your torch alerts the scanning spider-webs
and the movement-detecting dust
on the bottles in neat rows
aimed potently, oh, decades ago
directly at us; or laid down now
a vintage library of wine
when all the ferment is over, the promise
sealed in, these rare volumes
with rain and sun and wind in every chapter –
for the grape is a weather-gauge. Devour them!
They're Braille for the lascivious tongue
or distillers of metaphor for the smooth connoisseur,
every insight cross-referenced, interconnected.

from Album of Domestic Exiles (1996)

HEDGEHOG

Take these ingredients: Pacific darkness,
withdrawn hibiscus, a moon, once dusted
by volcanic ash, now attending lawns,
worms, snails, insects; a smorgasbord

for the nocturnal wanderer who,
baked in clay, was a dish himself,
some villagers' prey, the scoop of flesh
leaving name intact, and well-served here

by the night. Hedgehog. A surprise to find
him snouting clear of hedges and yet no visitor
to these unfamiliar, sprinklered grounds.
Hog: the word travels freely, changes

its meaning, sticks like wet insulting clay;
plays in the minds of the New Zealanders
who brought these spiny companions here,
though not jauntily to pursue shifting

perceptions of an epithet or a name.
This land's unstable, which means, hedgehog,
continued change; yet shorter hibernations
stress a correlation with the climate.

PROFIT AND LOSS

Witness this interior made of astonishing air –
invisible stairs, in case of fires, and a creaking lift
whose presence tightened phobics' throats; eight imagined floors
the width of a city block and subdivided
into rooms where typewriters clattered out insurance
policies to those whose ghostly names are free

of the sharp, annual responsibility to play
it safe and send a cheque; the accounts are windswept;
where memos flew, gulls, blessed with subatomic guile
encounter walls that are not there, swoop through
and up beyond the roof, a perch of air; the absent –
minded managers, sportsmen all, have blown their cover

and can't be seen though it's still early afternoon,
or the secretaries in mini-skirts, their shoes
kicked off, or the generation neatly seated
and parading blouses which included wives
for whom cigar-smoke rose with the stateliness of a bloom –
all lost to this wide athenaeum of profit and loss.

Yet as a shell it echoes while I dare summon
these patient rumours of a period, freed like wrack
by process, among mirror-glass storeys set
to disport the speed of light: the sky's the limit.
Unless a steely order slows the pace
like a set of brakes and so, with small pretence,

makes time-travellers of all who linger
and find nothing's changed but a careful
coat of paint. Like a film-set; yet
already cranes begin their art where nothing thrives,
and the graders – there's something playfully
absurd in the return like nomads of builders' labourers.

Or it is crisis; architect doubling as taxidermist
to oversee this vivid block, soon to be no longer dust-choked,
till it shines with heated, furnished floors –
its span dependent on a crane that waves its load
above the shuffling street and then, beyond these limits,
on what's claimed or copied or constructively made afresh.

BLOTTER

The past's a clean sheet
slipped into the present

for you, spotless servant,
who can no longer submit

to what's dripped or writ.
Hooked on speed, the ballpoint's

no pleaser, so I wish you dreams –
of full ink-bottles in desks

and libidinous pens;
of promiscuous Quink,

red, blue and green;
of encounters beneath sheets

of calligraphy.
There are memories a Parker

with a full bladder could share –
blotches and smudges,

your fêted recall
of wet cursive script

detectives could magnify
into a plot. Now

the blood of each pen
simply dries as it's shed, yet,

still fit to respond,
you guard each pad

from Basildon Bond.
Does this predict

the return of the nib?
Alas, a word is a word

whether processed or penned
and each submits to the view

this partnership's at an end;
which finds you in a bind –

so pure and utility-free,
the first sheet to be greeted

and the last to leave;
and that seems a drag. Still,

there can be comfort
in unsullied lag,

and within the security
of a new luxury pad.

A PAINTER IN PARADISE

Here is a bungalow where someone lived,
strict thatch and weave on a bamboo frame
returning to earth: the forest's food.
This is where the odd writer came, freelancing
on a holiday, proffering whisky
to the expatriate artist whose name
had brought to some galleries exotic charm.
"A Painter in Paradise" a fit
title for the feature with glossy pics.
By this pink frangipani he'd pose
in his blue sarong and, but for the grog,
wished them gone, he'd say, at his warung.
This is where he painted pretty boys
and occasional women, delighting,
a keen critic said, in the paint's seduction
of those with innocent eyes whom sadness tempted.
This is where he made his name. This is …
Ah yes, it's too hot to stay, and the slow
digestion of this place by rains
is all consuming, refusing to indulge
his fall — spreadeagled like a drifter
on the steps among the ubiquitous
rats and bats, the short-wave on, while elsewhere
gossip slyly unfurled beside potted ferns.

WILLOWS

For company, each other. Monkish, these stooped willows
huddled around the dam are guests when, at dusk, the rest
of the party has fled; guzzlers like their mates
whose reflections all day brisk rivers have trawled;
experts when the diviner discovers in the forked switch
he's grasping a seizure from water like lightning.
Look back, and they are tea-chests spurting leaves
in dumps by the Thames; social-climbers shading the Cam.
Fence-posts, bats: once I found shoots in a fencepost as true
as barbed-wire, spooks: and a caution for the man at the crease.
To wit, willow's brief is to picture what's been. A tree?
As surely as fire can sleep in leaves. It's males here that spread;
shadowy groups who, as if sunned by their fables, expand
whenever the land, also tireless, answers a sob in the wood.

TYPHOON

Heavy air, a tennis ball might stall mid-flight,
yet now at home, still in her whites,
she sees the dragonflies dart and freeze
outside the windows as if this proves

the forecast right. Familiar unfamiliar signs:
a ferry, unleashed and jaunty, from Kowloon
seems to mock the height from which she sees
the streets named for a colony

as if on a screen, since later cloud
must wipe this view clean. It is like flight.
The airconditioning makes a cocoon of home
with its bedrooms, withdrawn and patient,

the length of postcard-perforated school terms.
Those windows need checking too, for what is coming
could unsettle the Batik bedspread,
the didgeridoo; no stranger threat

than the cobra she's glimpsed some afternoons,
or the maid who, rattled, makes all the precious
glasses ping in mimicry of Cantonese.
She holds her calm like opened mail

postmarked Hampstead or Battersea
where "I'm home!" in a husband's voice
might fail pale rooms and engender sameness.
Here sampans cluster in the harbours.

Soon lightning teases. Collusion, it seems,
with days that flicker on the edge of China
seen through Peak windows clear as the borders
this change must shake. Can this date her praise

of such a view while time like coffee percolates?
Kites circle, distantly, upon neutral air –
calm elevated into daring; a shift of light
foreboding wind to which the closer trees will cling.

1992

ENVOY

Salt, seepage, reefs —
swing the champagne, now let this vessel
greet them as it shudders

down the slipway.
A thousand years its makings
have mellowed in a forest.

Think of those timbers
and imagine wine deepening
its flavour in a cellar,

longevities, hoardings,
adverse weathers. Pine
of pines, a Huon log

may loll for decades in a bog
and remain itself
though the timber-cutter's

name is earth —
a sustaining background
for a boat. So,

let it float, sail out
to sea, away, away
from its meeting with archaeology.

HAUTE LOCALE

This is Greene Street: sun and plants
    on a tar-black roof
from which, once, Ellis Island
    might have been guessed

through innocent fog. Her patch –
    the dark-eyed cosmetician
who for heights of her life
    commands the top floor, where,

in the sublet part, I'm a guest
    stretched gratefully
on the studio sofa.
    Oh America, her presence

makes you ever so much my neighbour
    and proves, as days go by,
such relationships become
    more complicated.

Dear US of A, I can't respect
    some things you do in the name
of power, and confess to being rude
    in a vulnerable mood.

Close up, things change, especially
    her Latin skin that's
passed ancestrally through Ellis Island
    to here, via Brooklyn.

This is post-war stuff, well-known
    elsewhere. But does
this beauty know about ozone
    depletion, the greenhouse

effect? She does, it seems, and makes
    a buck from oils and such
while her outdoor glow
    comes from staying in.

But it improves! The women
    she serves who appear to be
all of seventeen are the ones
    who are, astonishingly,

a ripe forty-three. And so I guess
    that's enough to convert
my languid view that what's clearly evident
    should also be true.

Ah, generous ally, home of the free
    cliché, now I'll sing
your star-spangled praises
    and you can guess what I mean.

If what I mean in Greene Street
    amid this looking-glass chic
allows for the converse of the converse
    of praising what's cosmetic.

THE PLEASURE SEEKERS

It's Friday night – if it's not Tuesday or Thursday –
and quick dusk is dropping its net on the first mosquitos,
the practised, pleading eyes of children with hands
outstretched for a few rupiahs; the carvings of no significance;
and from the beach, where waves mark time,
sunset richly blazes like a tourist brochure.
Sling the towel, seek release beneath accurate bats
who treat the place as if it's their own, and ignore
the stink of open drains nobody bargained for.
Return to the hotel, bar and pool – let the fun continue.

The Oxbridge Englishman, who lives in Paris,
affects an exit; the bald Frenchman, dressed in a tan
fitted annually since, well, long before the hordes started
coming loudly in more ways than one, retires to sulk.
Ah, Kuta Beach, you've survived the Dutch, the Japs
but not this invasion now demanding drinks
and planning another assault on the pleading streets.
The house-boys run the length of their remaining
open smiles to satisfy their clients' every whim.
Here's beer. Here's steak and chips. They feel at home.

Take off that acoustic music (it sounds religious!)
and let them get into some rock 'n' roll: the night explodes
and ease, that might admit the place itself, is ruined
though the absorbent heat continues to soak up random boasts
of thrills that have stretched each night to fraying point.
And what if this happened – the cloak of darkness broke
to reveal nothing, endlessly, but the unseen gecko's
emphatic, baffling cry in the bungalow roof?
Quick, quick, rejoin the group that's gathering now,
or lover, husband, wife. Live for the body. Eat and drink ...

Now time's a fast percussionist for those with bags
stuffed to their zips, whose flight darkness will swiftly
swallow but admit, the Frenchman fears, another charge
from where vulgar office-blocks, yards and homes collude.

Another bus arrives, is waved at, goes. The hibiscus sleeps.
Bodies regroup. The hours go on and must be devoured
as keenly as a gourmet's dish at knock-down price.
C'mon, they say, the night's still young, let's hit the piss!
Dark eyes watch them stalking shadow-like across wilted offerings
that might be refuse, towards the insomniac, throbbing bars.

VOYAGE

> *In 1618, a group of orphaned and destitute children left Britain for Richmond, Virginia in the United States. It was the start of an extraordinary era in British history, formally referred to as Britain's child migration scheme ... The final boatload left in 1967 when ninety children left Southampton for Australia ...*
>
> Lost Children of the Empire
Philip Bean and Joy Melville

Home windows again: gum trees
fired with noonday light scorch jet-lag
as, my case unleashed, I raise your
framed photo, mother, in black and white,

a pre-war girl I couldn't know;
rehearse your place beside the boys,
tanned and cheerful in their tennis gear.
Those attentive eyes, the half-formed smile

startle an inner voice till, suddenly,
it seems you might attend to speech:
though stubble's reflected in the glass
it is company I now congregate.

*

The quay, the heat, an officer
muttering "English scum" as I swayed
out of Immigration, still at sea,
baffled by my loss of cap till

"Barnforth!" and my outfielder's catch
restored, amid the crush, a neat
identity – while behind us the ship,
grey as winter skies, froze all exits.

One boy, out of sorts all voyage,
gave a cheeky Churchillian V.
Another spat at one who blubbered.
Hilarity when a seagull shat

on Miss Beecham, Sketchley-fresh.
Peachy, I didn't say. "Line up, children!"
Riff-raff, she meant. I could have burst
while the photographer arranged

our squinting and walked
the tripod like some antipodean creature –
till we were steady as a choir
about to lubricate an anthem.

             *

Awake amid the snores and stirring:
I'd lie in bed, one of twenty,
repeating the overland bus's
curves and bumps as headlights frisked

our ghostly faces till, from the wheel,
"Off yer arses, it's the farm"
verified the months' old lie –
this was no holiday, or else a dream.

Cold by then, you see, a habit formed
like wanking, grasping the miles
for clues of me. Oh soon enough
I would hear an iron bed-ends sing,

a prelude with odd magpies, while dawn
sure as the work of donnish vision
brought, for twenty instruments,
our "mother's" spoon percussion.

Lucky Wilkins, I thought, who was hard
of hearing, until there were bets
as to whether his pallid cheek
would be backhand red before

or after this, our "cottage", had been swept —
as if no former speck of Hartlepool
or Hove or Harwich must compromise
the bright, perpetual morning.

*

I kept my head down. Who'd rise
to meet the eyes of magnanimous
authority? Shovel, pitch-fork, pick —
lance-like, when out of sight, for play;

hands primed as sunbleached sheepskin,
proof, as on parchment, of instruction.
Out there, it might have been Africa
if galahs and possums hadn't betrayed

it as New South Wales — dwarfed as we were
beneath the wide continental sky.
The empty Empire! In the early sixties.
There, your son, in dungarees

claiming the brute, uninstructed sod
or blanching, once, to see a blade
in the soap-smooth hands of creepy Jones,
slit a sheep's throat as its hindlegs

jerked the blood out, spurt to torrent,
until, on the dust, it seemed all joy
had burst and made, soon enough,
a counterfeit of saying grace.

*

Let's be retrospective: upon Jones,
the creep, I confer a Ph D
in Philanthropy since he made
a mission, not out of place

among the institutional chores
and corridors, of being cold
as charity. "Fuckin' orphans!"
I once heard him blurt, as swaying

into sight he gripped a pin-up
as a drunkard might an amazing quid.
On each face, as if obedient
to his favoured rote, a bright "Who me?"

          *

Other contraband: a tranny.
Out in the paddocks, which ever
blazed half-way to nowhere, our ears
would lean to voices, songs, as if

for signs of habitation
on a planet. Christ! Some days Garner
could be forgiven for answering back
"It's nowt but a bloody race-track."

The caller's prattle like the sermons
suffered in the worldly whitewashed
chapel. Home boys. Tuning in
for word of where a correspondence

might exist – however tinny
R G Menzies' fruity guarantees.
Unless skyward blazed the Beatles' hits
out of somewhere Garner guessed.

          *

To venture further felt extreme.
After how long? Secretly reading,
beyond all chores, I colluded
with firm Miss Willis. It seemed always.

Now suddenly I'm rarely privileged,
bearing news of monthly fads
from bright, bisecting streets around
a country school. Oh, surely proud

you would have been to hear, in class,
"Jimmy Barnforth, a little louder,
repeat that answer to the room again."
My name! My name! Strange to say

it felt certificated, claimed.
Or else, one day, each kid on tape
reciting verse, shock of the stranger
with the Pommy voice. Guffaws

and goadings. Praise. Ever to play
the Home boy, or change. Yet no test,
in white shorts, with a ball could better,
"Repeat that answer to the room again."

*

Ah, transitions! Near that day
the rattling bus's brakes jammed, pound
sped to dollar. All change. Free,
I'm thinning soles toward the chores,

prepared to vanish where cheap mirrors
in a boarding-house will greet
rebellious hair and rout, at once,
the purity of the rural life

as will a gun-shot an expanse
of rabbits. For career. A softy's life!
Mint tokens of it nesting in my pocket
as, unhitching the farm-gate, I name

"Shakespeare," "Marlowe," "Raleigh," "Milton,"
grey god-damned buildings in the sun.
I'll say, "There's more from where these came."
Coins stalled on each palm like a brand.

*

Now whose currency drives Garner,
Wilkins, and the rest? Farm-hands,
at first, last coinage, imperial
investments spent. Mother, could you

have banked on this for me? Lost years,
a long conspiracy – each old
school tie of our Alma Mater real
as scrap baling twine. Thus attired,

I should pose before your photograph,
rescued from a living relative,
and shout, "Jimmy Barnforth, parent!",
soft hands, smell of airline soap,

transient as you in this sudden heat;
loosen, unknot it from my collar,
shagged as from a weekend saving hay,
to hang high as any twine upon a fence.

DÉNOUEMENT

When he copped his retirement package it was time
to leave the house with the cat and enter a dream:
passport, tickets for two, a failsafe scheme
to lick, in six weeks, each European shrine.
"It's a bit of a rush," she said, meekly alarmed.
He jabbed. "The kids did it at speed, so why not us?"
Twenty hotels, a barge, an airconditioned bus
youthfully shooting the rapids of an autobahn
provided windows for his supply of film;
room for varicosed legs and a conqueror's airs
(if not a consumer's). So, who really cares
what they praised – fashion in Paris, frescos in Rome –
or what they left stalled in the past. Now they're back;
and he's drilling and painting, sealing a crack.

from ALBUM OF DOMESTIC EXILES

LPs

If music hadn't stunned them
they'd be less upright
and orderly, confounded
by the echolalia of usurpers;
and slipping free of the rack,
welcome a spin away
from Coventry. To twist,
jive, rock 'n' roll, to samba,
mambo and waltz, to jig
jitterbug and jump, limbo
and swim, shake and shimmy;
take a break in a decade
of their own making
amid quiffs and stray hair
not in this unmarketable
glare of their absence,
a coup d'état of the air.
Twelve inches of stalled
reckoning while their minder
got stoned on a riff –
Ah stiff! Party-goers,
they always skipped a beat
or swerved from the track,
and space they claimed
as a right, when memory thins,
is better claimed back. Exile's
an eclipsed disc parade
when a die-hard fad's sacked.

Sahib

Gastronomically, I beg:
keep away from my table
the seditious ratatouille
(it blows-out my braces);
curry not, in this dotage,
to my years as Sahib;
stall like a new-issue uniform
the sushi or sauerkraut,
all the dishes that follow
a foreign *s* to my bib.
Let me fart with abandon;
let me be an old goon
for unabridged versions
of Mrs Beeton and the force
in thrifty stewed prunes.

Mussolini's Umbrella

For now the umbrella
will be banned from the house
as a traitor to rugged
complexions. *Ombrello* –
little shadow; too cute,
mused Il Duce, amid
this century's downpour
of bullets. It rises
abruptly as the national debt
and parades street to street
as a weakness. Let there be
hailstorms, heat, thunder
like jackboots striding
terrible skies; let
them bravely flush-out
from cupboard or carboot
this conspicuous wretch
which given speech and
a dig in the ribs might confess
his dandy cheek is the
similitude of *a rose*
or a peach. Exile
this pansy to wasteland
or the muteness of movies;
seek it if it's stalled
in a cavernous hallway
like a tropical bat –
for it is the downfall
of national weather
and shelters a shadow
where there should be a lout.

Absent Third Party

Reader! Everywhere there are signs
of me: bud, fossil, seed, galaxy,
though now I'm a future riddle
within a playground of quarks
while, skimming the lines of a book,
that shadow-like beard scans
the look on your face. Can you hear
a thrum on your eardrum?
I dance. I sing. To you I bellow
my neat autobiography, rising star
on the horizon: here's me having a fling,
and next I upstage the solar-system.
Book-lover, does not your eye
now twinkle? At this location
ovum after ovum, big as suns,
outdistance me; have got the drop
on that limp member wintering out
each book you thaw on a double-income.
I am patient. Strong. But mostly
like the buff of a book club I need
the means to belong. Look,
a book must belittle a DINK
when it replaces a condom –
won't you rise and circulate now
as a breeder? Give those pages
the brush-off! Let me too be a reader.

LONG DISTANCE

The phone is casual when it conveys
a loved but disembodied voice, astray
in generous galactic hiss, hang the expense.
It's not like talking across a table, for the split
second delay enjoys vast distance, call it

ocean and desert interference. There's night,
here's day, clever the way the satellite
ignores them, and the lands where missiles
sit poised to reinforce invective.
It's strange to be so blind but so receptive.

Dial again. Now the voices come clear, oh so
recently close, it seems ear rests on ear to show
distance has thinned, time zones twinned ...
or just that home is all places to the telephone
with its fluent and garrulous dial tone.

FIRST TASTE

I'm recalling clear skies, and the voluted calls of magpies;
and those eucalypts, rinsed, quivering, fresh
in the early light you stepped into from the pickers' hut

where sleeping bags lay discarded like skins.
We headed for the strawberry rows, hair wet from the shock
of cold water, where stacked punnets were a threat

of work. It made you feel lazy, estranged,
knowing the future – whole days, a couple of weeks –
was parallel rows like rails to stoop over.

Work, the first taste of it; it was tempting to sidestep
and bolt home to holiday idleness
but instead we'd begin, again,

and doggy forward: blindly competitive.
Get going early, before the sun seemed
harsh as a lash on our backs, and the boss,

a Seventh Day Adventist, came to stand behatted
in the distance, powering his silence among trees.
Look up, assess, move on. It was like exposing

choice secrets. Some berries were revealed
to the sun like our noses, shiny, reddened and pointed;
and then the freeing of stalks like pulling out corks.

Others were fat, happy, a whole juicy mouthful.
Feel under the leaves, and there damp lingered
with slugs, snails, and whatever wandered onto that job

which, as row after row conceded,
included those lithe adolescent dreams,
nourished or repelled by touch, fruitfulness, exertion.

There were shy berries also, curiously white,
safe from our fingers' seduction. The rest
caused temptation, hand to mouth collusions,

until gluttony, ballooning our stomachs,
made wind of that bounty – left each of us,
punnet by punnet, to learn the strict value of money.

THE PEDANTS
for Leah

It's the A3072 through Devon
and our course is accurate
past trees massed
in the discerning shade
of my daughter's eyes –
chestnut, birch, beech.
"Lovely," I say, "a forest."
"Woods," she says, five emphatic
years safely in the back seat
as we glimpse brilliance
poked into the leafy
tunnel we're burrowing
through. But now,
past farms, I counter with "woods"
as the car discards a cape
of shadow. "No, forest!"
and her eyes, playful, pace
long seconds as if they
could attend the furthering
of the trees' rings until,
on higher ground, I'm
in loose sympathy
with the odd, demonstrative
oaks that on this land
shade a spreading claim
to where a forest was. And so
along roads dappled with pedantry
she like a sapling switches
to "Well, just a bunch of trees"
which roundly sees off another lot
now that, across open country,
the coast's appeared. In *satin* light?

SHOE DOLL

A poor child's doll from London –
Museum of Childhood, Edinburgh

After all there was life without the streets,
slogging to factory or grocer's stall,
till rainwater crept in like debt, spurred
this shoe into further comfort. London,
thanks to your stiff, apparelled citizen
propped upright, now, for swift inspection,
we know how moonlit terraces nursed
ingenuity after hours – a step back
or forward into love's rehearsal. Weird:
brute leather assuaged by a small apron, dress;
talk about kick up a fuss (she must have),
ridiculous in its servant's frilly cap.
Here, in posterity's heaven, stripped
of care – arms rocking her to chilly sleep –
she outstares pride and pity, rapt pretence.
Her name, can we guess? Victoria, Jane …
All's ignorance. Our eyes remake her; or else
with those spindly arms of wool-bound wood
she's the factotum of remembered toys.
Her rags make them shine and fashion loss.
Ah, what a perverse, historical kindness
has made of her a gift like a bruise
from cobbler's nails. In her service
the vanquished, imperial childhoods quail.
Pretty dolly! Ugly? No. Those epithets
not ours to give would claim her now like touch
once making rags and leather sleep –
scrap features, heel for a face; there's nothing
more she'd bawl or break-up for than pretence.

TAKING MY DAUGHTER TO THE CAVE

Outside it's the New World; clean air,
damp ferns; an entrance surprised by loggers
toppling the future one afternoon,
its thunder, ground shudder, ours for keeps.

The blackness theirs. It takes a guide,
flick of a switch, to scare with light
the million-years-old cave monster, fear,
and hear it trickle like a stream

through rock fissured, sure enough,
by continental drift, to where
no proto life-form shows the way.
Here might big questions arise again.

Should it seem more strange to hazard
answers underground than in the car
or leaf-strewn street where progress
derides what's out-of-date? My sweet,

my kid, my china plate, there might
have sprung a revolution in fast-food or
linguistics while, amid cave
spiders and beetles, we're diverted

by a stalagmite whose lit growth,
in a century, you'll shame within
a week. We hear its name. Well,
that's affectionate, tamed as stars.

Or echoes. Voices. Curiosity.
So lead us, comrade, past formations,
"The Wedding Cake," "Tower of Pisa,"
or whatever tricks the light proposes.

THE CONCEIT OF GLASS
Murano, Venice

Of course there is display of stock-in-trade –
glasses, ashtrays, regiments of figurines
cooling swiftly into feverish cash; out of sight
the glass-blower aims his pipe into the air
and swells the melt, spins it like a circus prop.
All day the glowing orbs are schooled to act
their parts in deepest space where heat seems less
a case of sweat than the gauge confirming it.
Like the tongs, it never stalls; a furnace mimics
the flow of some volcano; in sympathy
the glassware ever moves in constant queues –
kind with kind, to distant houses, the conceit
of each conceded by the renegade few, skewed
as tree-roots, true to a planetary, wilder heat.

DAYS OF INCOMPLETION

It is the morning of the job still-about-to-be-done –
the garden fork holding the soil in its place
like an hors d'oeuvre. Meaning talk not action
characterises this season, and doodles (deciphered)
outwit tasks delivered like punishments. I ask,
did Capability Brown stand appalled when,
surveying his scape, its completion dismissed him?
It's the idea of foreplay that pleases, the flight
but not the arrival when, an undercoat applied,
the topcoat in its can for weeks merely teases.
Friend to such suspense is, praise be, undying breath.
Ah, days of incompletion – the umpteenth draft,
the road yet to be taken – I embrace them, let go.
Torpor of their obverse: a last nail's driven home.

from Russian Ink (2001)

NIGHTFALL

The leaves release their light.
Bees, the fuchsia's guzzlers,
quit their day routine as
somewhere a voice calls,
"Come inside." No need,
sitting here, to tame
the inside table's
fresh disorder. Or, going
further, mind whether
amid our silhouetted hills
you need elect blind chance
as the designer which offered up
the adapted fish
for dinner. Everything's
complete and steady
as rooftops beneath the stars:
the past and future
fold in the breadth
of all the air. Till wait –
now of a sudden, later,
it's all so lidded, silent
for no waking reason;
it seems a brink.
Unless it's a crater
one plummets into speaking
the town's two urgent syllables.
Then try repeating:
"Dark clouds over Siberia"
and "I write with Russian ink".

CARING ACCENTS

Thanks to research and dissemination
in the *Daily Telegraph*, it's confirmed
there are accents, ever remote
from speech's main street that inspire
trust and, therefore, customers
to set free as words their worthy quids.

To that end, service industries
might shift there or – it's not reported –
employees could just mimic the accent
of that region. It's true, we all
want to be cared for – even on the phone
when dealing with a firm

which given an opening (see
the fine print) will vanish through it.
Now, happily, the accent, fast echoing,
will be just for you. This is good.
The stereo's walked or, better, the house
is smoke and there's a caring accent

right on cue. Duw, Duw*, if concern's from Wales:
the choice of many. Or, if in this country,
where accents breach regional
sensitivities, a pause perhaps
while care germinates across the breadth
of a chosen State. It will vary.

The catch is, it just can't last.
Those favoured vowels, from some Appalachian saddle,
will be tumbled to or robbed. Soon,
the caring accents are duly gone. Unless,
to turn an honest dollar, they become
the ones that really cared all along.

* God, God

STORIES OF MY FATHER
J.G.S. 1912–1996

1 The Call

The phone rings, mid-evening,
a stray alarm now that he'd have downed
those salving Scotches after dinner.

A hemisphere away
from stories like difficult stains
on furniture steadying the half-drunk glass;
the dining-room dark around a lamp's
frugal shaft where, for decades,
his maths explored the page
while darkness, the equaliser,
found London or Melbourne to be much the same.

Then in that focus, a magnifying glass
at the ready, to find a line on
a world that's wide as print, or stalled
at golf scores, grammar, dates.

Mid-evening, impatient
during a favourite film, the phone's
singlemindedness commands obedience.

Now through the house,
it's death that's proved
never to be timely.

2 Personal Pronouns

As singular personal
pronouns go, we were close:
"I never see you do the washing up;"
"I have been ringing
but you've been out."

Then there was silence,
the intermediary, potent enough
to see if "I" would concede to "you."

Father and son, at the crossroads,
in a classic round of words,
pronouns circling undeclared verbs.

These the two words that stand accused.

Fixed in binary opposition,
they proved he could
never grow old nor I grow up.

I just wanted to get him off my back.
Now it's the certain weight I lack.

3 Stories

The same for families
as within countries: conflict comes
from telling stories.

We had that licked.
Great Events of the Twentieth Century
– world wars, migration –

and our family's part in them
devolved to his roomy equivocation;
night curtains drawn, Scotch doing its best

to free the people, places
I wanted most. Now
there's nothing to be said

except identity precedes
the parental bed like land,
affection, hate, the whole gang

of family with its clamour.
I'll never gee it straight, or wish to.
There'll not be his Scotch to intercede.

I am the sole beneficiary.

4 Good Liars

Photographs, for instance,
in which my mother and I
seem so composed. Looking now

at the cobbled streets or trees
it was a steady hand and sensible eye
that borrowed backgrounds

he couldn't know
would never match the facts.
Instability elsewhere

and *Amateur Photographer* each month.
Or there was strange light;
his camera an emigrant, unpacked

too late in 1962 ever again
to frame his wife
beside her boy.
    Spooled,
past use-by, his cache
of film matched every
holiday never taken.

5 Getting Through

Now I remember:
it was when there was a problem
with the TV antenna

the news reader didn't take
his place at dinner
and, long before the autocue,
make his eyes define

the reports as fair and true.
My mother's was the closest voice
our house, one afternoon, had lost.

I saw my father
getting through without a line
on why she'd swallowed
so many sleeping pills.

It was like no sound.
It was taboo as emotions
for readers of the news;
the mystery of Adults Only.

Soon enough, the mild-eyed
news reader improved.

The dilemma,
something to do with the likes
of tonight's electrical weather.

6 Telling Jokes

On a Cabcharge receipt,
for his granddaughters,
an ink sketch of a wounded bull.

Once, to see if I'd get it,
there'd been the joke
he'd heard at an office do.

It began, "This is a true story;"
and this is too: my retelling
is word for word the same.

Still I hear it – punchline, for laughter,
overdue. "Say it now!" I pleaded.
It was too good to be true.

7 Summing Up

All the figures that equalled death,
my father, an actuary, assessed
and put his own probability on the shelf.

Till, at fifty, there's only his or my
funeral to prove death's case
and keep him from his laden desk.

Death had its own policy
of carrying his family off
and left him calculating, against the odds.

Of white coats and stethoscopes he was shy –
pain an abstraction such omens
might elect to call his own.

The best medicine, post-surgery,
at eighty, banishment of doctors.

My father was a lasting figure.

8 Immortality

I tried to follow
in my father's footsteps
once, at his golf club.

Then there's the flag at half-mast,
drinkers at the bar, telling stories to get a grip
on how his aberrant swing never
influenced his firm opinions

about other players at the tee.
If with confidence I'd said it was
his way of overcoming vulnerability,
habit of mind, a legacy
of boarding-school scholastic heights
that groomed a singular view,
turned stubborn under threat,
as when he stashed the English language
in mid-century London deep-freeze,
or found advice to imply a compromise
of his own good counsel even when,
half-blind, he aimed his car,

they might have discussed
how all or none of these
(nothing certain in his game)
allowed him, within a week,
two holes-in-one
in perfect collaboration
with an offshore breeze.

DOWN FROM MARS

Mostly you know where things come from –
pumice, bills, heartache, seasonal rain
or the shearwaters back from Japan;
and then there was the meteorite
without a source. Black days.
I think of it. Alien. Metaphor
for a state of mind where book or breadth
are strange. Dropped, one morning,
into Egypt – a challenge, at least,
to the pyramids. This is a challenge:
getting through, with little wonder.
This orb, a focus, solid now
and odd as trying to place
the stranger in the mirror. So it goes
for this excursion through dark days
where those companions who can't
connect disappear. A rock will do.
What brought it down to earth
was clever: a Martian meteoric
impact. Could I stand it? Already
there've been enough disruptions.
I aim for the square root of events
or calculate when science beamed
the way to its nature. Viking mission '79.
Mars and back to Earth with matching evidence.
If now I could grasp the source
of this darkness when the sky is bright,
far-fetched as that marvellous rock
whirled a million million miles
free of Martian gravity, the future
round the house might seem less a threat.
Ah, throw open the windows to ontology,
space to shake off this state – whoever
collected that desert rock guessed
there'd need to be explanations.

THE QUESTION AT A STATION

What if … ? you say, claiming a hair
off my shoulder as the moment
for the train gets nearer. Amid the din
the speculation drifts,
                            unformed,
as it has before on a schedule
of its own where there's
no taxi ride or hotel room

though light, right for the season,
slants through the window,
brightens queues of books.
Letters arrive. Someone knocks.

Entrances and exits everywhere –
like there, where you are,
and I, suddenly, am not;
already distant from the question's
pause that forms a country
where among the millions
there's just two people
and, in the balance, neither
an election nor a seismic aftershock.

It puts you on the spot.
Amid the noise, the coupling
and uncoupling of trains

not to have any say seems fateful.
The rails gleam over and over,
curved as the world, between alpha and omega.

This is how far the question's got.

THE SKIN'S REACHES

Seamless as heat
skin's the full stretch,
my tongue, tasting
her body at earlobe or neck, wets;
only then is she truly undressed.

Sweats: a tropical
fest. In bed's
a journeying back
to where first hominids
strayed amid waterfalls,
fruit, vaporous ways.

All's saltlick, expanse
this far from the coast.

Slithery skin suits us
best in such climate –
amphibious, boundless
as before boom-gates,
at old borders, shut out
the garbed
        who see
the way to go further

is the distance on sheets.

INDIAN PACIFIC

1

A dream I have: rails
stretching across seas,
then skyward to blue nowhere;
now these – flat out,
hard, across the continent
and I, as any dreamer,
am alone or hear passengers
pitched like parcels against
corridor walls as the train
sways though the wheatbelt,
shorn and complete.
If they are neighbours,
this is a street, on steel wheels.
Look, it sports cockatoos,
a team seizing trees;
now, in a huddle, wheat silos.
This thoroughfare as dream:
serial displacement. Going east,
after the dark, past distant
weathers: radiant cumulus,
thunderheads, epic sunshine.
Travel, this unravelling:
Merridin, Southern Cross, Kalgoorlie …
names for somebody's home;
count them to sleep. Stellar,
they might seem from above,
migrating matter winking
tribally in the black (at dusk
I hitched, as a student, out
of Broken Hill by plane
and saw it as a lit Titanic
slowly tilting down) but
sleepless, I'm inclined to repeat
Indian Pacific, Pacific, Pacific …
Dawn's wheeling distances

locate this train as an axis
which, after the blaze,
bites the rails briskly,
since now, at the windows,
riffled blur is the foreground
and the engine speeds
as if shovelling, fast-forward,
miles of gibber like a miner
tunnelling toward space;
or else, as the eye strays,
squat saltbush is gradual
mid-distance. For this trip
is domestic: minimised risk;
and across bedrock limestone
favours long retrospection
of a past occupant, ocean,
where it's still all blue
Above on this Below of plain –
a geological dry run
for the train's haste, parting
sides, audacious as a fence.

2

Call this a vantage, against
the westering sun, and I view
progress into a noun
autocracy: Nullarbor.
After a stop, in my pocket,
blanched limestone, ruddy granite
will relay the one name
at home, on a shelf, tamed;
the thoroughfare of the train
a long approach, as travel is,
to where home lies as a choice
or circumstance, proved;
and there, look, as a hat
graces a stand, a raven,
electing both, nests on the one

post for miles around;
on its own schedule; eggs
the colour of opals.
Those stones that bloom
on finger and pendant
here, in the carriage, as the sun
angles in — and there's talk
of other journeys, swapped
like souvenirs, precious
and condensed. The Indian Pacific
an aisle for strangers to merge
into a community that requires,
for its open exchanges,
rhythm and bounce
of the breadth of Australia —
its uninhibited horizontals.
Lunar tyre-tracks there;
litter of glass where thirst,
unassuaged, has exploded it.
This speed: territorial; coast
to coast, controlled
as a celluloid film unreeled;
or, as a steward from the city
would agree, repetitive
as all-night TV. Each
window showing what's on:
mallee conceding to myall
over a thousand miles;
ochreous sandhills; sun.
A landscape for freight
or calendars, sound:
the long air-conditioning,
placental, hums dutifully
of towns. Home. Recalled dreams,
some steamy summer night,
of spaces such as these —
suspended disbelief needed
now you are astray in space-time
or in a tight squeeze.
Till, out of sleep, beyond glass,

again there appear trees,
full-scale; birds, breeze —
your heartbeat, the first
and last open signal
down this long corridor east.

WAITING GAMES

Waiting, too, needs a strategy
as artists do, heads askew, gazing
like the commuters, here, in cold air.

So many faces in appointed tension:
puffed, pale, ashen, sanguine.
As a child you knew this was scheduled,

the prayer-cushion, your knees,
in opposition. Built-in like blood:
be patient. Try imagining the job

of the bloke in blue: his house, his books.
Or the bun-eater who reminds you
– of who? – the way she stands.

Name eight varieties of potato. Glue.
The child who streaks the length
of the station, screaming, displays

one variety of waiting that is,
after all, there to be inhabited
like wrinkles. The numbers equate

elsewhere, if the train continues
overdue, which – let's not be extreme –
could cause exponential waiting

beginning here and moving out
(no refuge there from bonhomie),
porch-lit house affecting house

throughout the metropolis like a virus.
Now, to calculate its speed, count
those already present. Nobody move.

WALKING ALONG AN ESTUARINE SHORE
for Tim Burns

Mud flats here: low tide. A cormorant
fishes off a rocky cape where the last
of a logger's jetty rots. Sombre light.
These are lines for paintings made abstract
and elegant so each ramifies more
than if some greedy brush sequestered
the scene, complete, and stored it – ripple
of water, a bone picked clean, the rim
of estuarine hills cleared of names.
I walk along the primeval shore
where pebbles are smoothed by tides
and recall your paintings, the given
weather-driven forms, light sensitive,
as if amid the changes they shadow
a hinted blueprint. Egg shapes, rectangles too –
and already the light has changed, defining
fossils in shattered rocks like coins recovered,
announcing and renouncing empires.
Upon tiny crabs, beneath the boulders,
my footsteps pound. The tide sucks back.
Mud, rock made of mud, footprints – mine –
firm as paintstrokes: all there is to show
that here someone shaped the light and saw,
between the banks, a water-bird fly north.

GOLCONDA
for Freya

Where you don't live,
though signposts follow it
as compass needles do the Pole.

It's where, at dusk, the muezzin's
cry confirmed the hour
in the Sultanate

that began to make the name
synonymous with wealth
and power. A caught sun

of gold in the mosque's dome
and a diamond, big as an eye,
on the Sultan's finger.

A sort of rising Tokyo
of the sixteenth century.
A tented army already

riding towards
wealth's centre, its elixir,
to do what's done by other means

in a democracy, I think,
as you, my daughter,
speed north through open country

– farms, declining towns –
on the road where ravens,
stripping carrion, indolently

flap clear of wheels.
Till there's a turning
that wanders (unfold the map)

to where Golconda, Tas.,
is clearly shown. Your rendezvous
for the festival that'll quit

the one half-settled street,
flush with all it can expect
of its sequestered name.

RED EYE

The bloodshot eye
and the good one that return my gaze
from the mirror, guide me
to the eye clinic;

its generously sized
waiting room, a confession:
the complaints are many;
and like a dog

cornered by threat, I stare,
unblinking,
at the company
I now keep the length

of my waiting. Far
into the room with veiled windows
and prints – by an artist
with decorative flair –

I see the whole assembly wears glasses,
familiars of blur
like an inversion
of the ocular

process that made,
amid rank swamp,
primal membrane bud into light,
and at last has brought us,

marvellous-eyed
– once! – to the beige
and sage green decor
of the clinic, for correction.

Darkness, or, rather,
absence of light, will have
its way again, waits
as patiently. Unless

like a worm
suddenly unearthed, I squirm
amid the slickly
serviceable decor

and lousy magazines
(some are freed from reading) –
a collective test
when a mere bug can pick

a real leaf from plastic!
Let there be cathedrals,
great paintings, the night sky
emptying its light, all

a reward for my good eye;
and let the other
soon again offer proof
of the Argument from Design.

A SHOWER MEDLEY

Behind frosted glass,
a naked woman in profile
lifts hair off her neck.

This might be a film
and she's probably
Juliet Binoche.

Those who'd prize this scene
would pack a bathroom
the size of a stadium

as I too would prove
just how foolish it might
be to loiter in steam

and document the social
implications of showers.

*

Between night and day
between naked and neat
between sweat and a wedding
between fucking and cooking
between stalling and school
between Aussies and Poms
between books, between jobs
between fire and flood
between taps, at 45°
between bills, quarterly
between here and eternity
falls the shower, full steam
in the chi-chi ensuite.

*

Tropic maker, rainy season,
at the turn of a tap; gravity's
straw in the wall; year after year,
saluter of tiles, country-wide,
(till one of the legion cracks up);
bighead obsessed with any angle
on extraterrestrial matters;
to the power of households,
firm as a pledge – mad gadget,
above the need for a mandate.

*

Don't think
because its heat's
so loyal

to the contours
of my body,
that I'm not aware

with Heraclitus
one cannot step into
the same shower twice.

This dictum I praise
when the temperature plummets
in the bath.

*

Upright again and lost in steam
I lather soap and blink:
here's to waking, flip-side of dream;
time again to think

or listen to the FM band,
being careful not to slip,
or sing too loud, or simply stand
and let the water rip –

for what's in dams isn't a spot
on flow when it's habitual.
Give me extremes of cold and hot
mixed in a mega-ritual.

SNAKE WORDS

From the north, a modest assembly of houses,
the snake catcher is coming. He will show
no fear and, if the newspaper's a guide,
will wear khaki, and smile. Let's understand,

I say, what the journalist means when she claims
he has "an affinity for" his creatures.
Or, yes, surely "with" them. Though their affinities
mock his, it's clear, to his advantage.

He's paid to save them from us. People.
This, a migrant English class. Refugees. Advanced.
The snakes and the snake catcher are language,
past and future continuous: he's committed

to the rescue of kitchen-raiding snakes
since, as he says, their gene pools suffer.
Like genocide but snakes, Fatima says. Well, yes.
Copperhead, tiger, black snakes. Venomous.

Tomorrow each will be here in class,
saved from our country, which saves twenty fares
to where the snake catcher's affinity
finds its share of deeds. For us, in tough hessian,

nouns, usefully of the concrete kind, at rest
or slithering with adjectives; hosting colours; touch.
Fear, the abstract killer, in close-up.
Though for that no plan to instruct is set.

MOTHS

1

Which come out at night
and collect next to the front door
might burn themselves out with excitement –

the light left on late for welcome
and safety, though it's a gothic enactment
from a midnight forest that greets;
strobe effects, rapid as eyelids blinking away
some irritant grain.

Not homely. The moths guess
it's the close glow of the moon that shows
the street number and door brass,
their guide in the place where
for millennia they've bred.

Now, wings spread on cream brick, they're exposed
to daylight's comings and goings. Look,
their intricate symmetry is striated
like bark. Brown, various as sediment
laid down however long they've outflown
the rush of eye and beak among leaves.
A dozen, fifteen, out of the shadows,
sharp against brick, like exhibits.
Going nowhere, out of place
at this address if it wasn't obvious
they show us where we live.

2

The street name I can't recall
or the house of my father's acquaintance
(whose name is lost) and least of all
the species of moth he

attracted with a light
whose beam at night seemed more apt
for international landings.

It's the amazement I retain –
the scurry and swirl of moths
caught in the glare like hurled flakes
from a blaze on Guy Fawkes night.

And the net. For, suddenly,
this brilliance had purpose. The moths were homing in to him,
his place, wherever that was –
decades and twelve thousand miles from here.
Out of the darkness a frantic silent film
of moths – which unlike planes
you'd watched, hopping searchlights,
couldn't dodge the opposition –
I'm recalling now since memory
comes increasingly to seem
a habitation.
         Caught,
beneath his thumb they twitched.
Then, to regiment species
beneath glass, he'd pin them down.

3

It is news around here:
moths exposed, identities pending;
far from Gypsy Moth, Tiger Moth, names
used as talismans to guide
ocean adventurer, trial pilot.

See, some we admire and adopt,
hoping for safety, out in the spaces
where everything's strange: long range.
Then there was Charles Darwin, loose, at twenty-two,
in the forests of Brazil.

This returns to me now, checked,
since old reading from memory bleaches.
Index: butterflies, moths. Curious –
of the latter few offered
themselves to his net. What
can we expect to remain
now so much, so quickly, such forests
are just print? Look: camouflage
is a means of exposure, there,
here, out of the trees, a late twist
for that clear-sighted naturalist

in the thick of taxonomies –
Anophylla magnifica, Macroneme immanans.
One tricks as bird shit, the other a wasp.

4

I pretend to be a tree.
I pretend to be invisible.
Or, adaptable, both at once
when in afternoon heat I accommodated
moths, a plague, millions
dropped from a clear sky
as a warning for civilians
or just my good luck, after school,
to be brave in hostile territory.

Luckier when young than, now, being host
to select moths next to the front door?
There is no such agent as luck, just conjunctions of events.

Luck is the darker form
of peppered moth, on black trunks,
with all the smoke and grime
of the Industrial Revolution to select it;

or light on this hill, shining late,
now all are home of a Saturday night,
where moths skirr like good odds
for a lottery already won.

5

There's change in any event –
the moths are testing the binary stakes,
ranging from dark toward light, a scattered archipelago,
at rest, here, weightless as images
gleaned from a book. View them away

from their relatives' domestic fame.
Check the clothes drawers, walk among graves;
ghouls and devourers, the visible world
gives them the creeps. Amid dissolution
their appetites stir: they can't live
with uncertainty, so cling to your skin.

For years ahead, in cupboards,
mothballs breathe. Let the air in, the wind.
Soon enough what's to come will stall
all reckoning: late-night arrivals; these
I've pinned down, in the museum –
Melanodes anthracteria, safe
where early sunlight defines them.

NORTHERLY

Too rough for fishing; we headed into the peninsula,
leaving the dinghy; rocky capes and bays
never far from the windscreen

or the elevated houses, corralled by pines,
with their steady fix on the ocean.
Toward all points of the compass

the tyres flashed gravel at the corners –
for the country is far north of here
where surveyors are bored by horizons that skim

the planet without hilly compromise.
On this day, a gusting northerly reminded us
of its magnitude: a rushing sound

of distant surf in the casuarinas;
a dinghy, crab-angled, roped to a ramp.
In a bleached paddock, rosellas

seesawing for seed. These
at a gear-change. By nightfall
the number won't be counted on fingers –

and the peninsula is wide open like a bird-map
taken back to the shack
I recall now, weather-gripped

in midwinter. At the roadside, wrens,
tails twitching forward like pens
then flight scribbling through bush.

North, or perhaps south, an eagle
hooked muscle from a tyre
pummelled possum. We stopped

to hear plover ratchet their shrieks
and see oystercatchers, among these,
red-beaked connoisseurs on the beach.

Then we knew why the little boat
didn't matter, how disappointment
is a hawk hovering above a hill,

and the vast scope of its survey
at this toe-end of the continent.
Flame robins, nearer, dots brush-thrown

amid banksias; herons, fine-hinged
to stalk in the shallows, and stab ...
and now in the tousled grevillia

a New Holland honey-eater,
no, two, and too late for nectar
— though not that day in the peninsula —

I'm watching, ruffled witness
on an unpredicted trajectory in bad weather.
Recalling, now, that earlier afternoon

the clear sky, heat, northerly wind
increasing, and nothing yet reckoned
about a boat and the unbidden species.

A FOOTNOTE ON TORTURE

Red skin on a thin wrist from the quick
twist of a Chinese burn, or else

there was the quarter-nelson,
an arm gripped by some bully, then skewed
back till, upping the pressure – his warm breath

on your neck – the only dignity left
was down to the chief position of prayer:

such boyish tortures I recall, half-fondly,
faced, some stuffed evening, with an American sitcom
or stalled, phone in hand,
with Muzak leaking through;

note that what I know
of the universal rack and screw

is mostly film and print,
a list with every
body-part a target,

given what a cigarette, bamboo, a rat can do.
Yet now find there's one other fact.

I know conception too –
for the way the awful list proves its ready extension

finds me barefoot and tortured
by an English Channel pebble beach,
assured a sunny jog (enforced)
would've made the SS quake.

BELLI'S SHADE

Guiseppe Belli, poet and Vatican censor, wrote over two thousand sonnets in the Roman dialect. He died in 1861.

1

Rome's terracotta roofs temper the light
of April, May or June though not the din
of traffic, or thundercloud homing in
from the Tyrrhenian; remain the height
Giuseppe Belli viewed – and here tonight
he graces his piazza, a decent win
for ribald blasphemy, the urge to sin
in sonnet form, and proof that flesh is right.
Which is to swear that in bronze he stands so tall
amid flirtation, whatever the racket
or black weather, our man was his shade, all
set to test lust's language; sex: cracked it,
word, clause and sentence, off a silent hall,
where theology's shed lightly as a jacket.

2

Not blessed with frescoes or bones of a saint –
the basilica's famous for its plainsong,
so he perched quietly amid the throng;
inner heaven, though outwardly it needed paint.
Minutes on, he knew. Desire fought restraint
soon as he saw her, dark hair, fair skin, strong
voice in a ritual now overlong
for a temporal evening the Pope might taint.
This reflection had balls; her friends were priests.
Drinks, she said, at my place. Yes. Already,
in the distance, Belli's statue stood as yeast
to expectation in these streets Blind Freddy
could see are rife with licence, west to east,
though her knees, so bare, in the car were steady.

3

He thought: how much in common there's to share
between Belli, Vatican censor, obsessed
by fleshly pleasure, loud taboos, expressed
in sonnets whose "fucks" rocked tavern air,
and him, cupboard poet, employed by Intercare.
Northward they sped, and the priests who blessed
the prospect of an evening drink, confessed
all were there engaged in theses. None, to be fair,
had found Belli. It's my mission, he vowed,
to redeem this lack even as, at her place,
booze was drunk and the discussion, loud,
was wide of her eyes, his, kindling that grace
which governs all, is urgent, deplores the crowd
when guests, outside a closet, affect the pace.

4

Above him, exalted, that later week,
since on his back he gained a better view,
a fresco of the Virgin, robed in blue,
was one position, swapped about, until each peak
released the lovers, breathless, cheek to cheek –
she wanting tea and he a smoke to woo
the room, that image, into focus few
fans of the Eternal City fail to seek.
This was perfect; though he quailed. It's said
(see Belli) there're more words in the Roman tongue
than any other for cock and cunt, read
or spoken. He'd not uttered one. Or sung
one either when, as they romped, she said: bed
sure trumps demotic verse. His balls, disheartened, hung.

5

In this state he skipped most of his Conference
devoted to third world nations, and she a swag
of theology lectures. Sex rejects as slag
long disputation, elects the present tense:
upside down or on all fours made greater sense
than bums on seats when homonyms, e.g. shag,
won street cred at her Lay Centre – jest and brag
as an address, he gasped, and vast its influence.
It wouldn't last; his flight out was swiftly due.
She, a fresco, shame, soon must concentrate
the minds of priests; meaning they'd hear, on cue,
the words of Belli, Anglo-Saxon and Latinate,
in loose translation – and of the statue
he'd vowed to show them, colossus, at a later date.

A WORLD WITHOUT CREATURES

Sailors, reaching port, are heard to say,
"Two weeks and we saw neither bird nor fish."

Great oceans, heaving. Liquid mountains. Days.
Till it's imagined we, hill and tree surrounded,

might fix our positions and foresee
strange watchful faces searching ours

for news and comfort, much as children gaze
into rows of Christmas shops. Suddenly, we're alone.

For though flagpole, spire and signpost
confide real bearings, no compass will attract

the ground-bird, insect, snake or bat
any more than, out of the ark, will stumble

a cartoon leaf-eater to retrace
its journey to water on a fossil track.

Thank goodness for photographs
of cub and chimp but, ah, how sentimentality

falls short of dodging, beneath abundant starlings
abundant crap. To wit, a nuisance stain

now is remembered as an honorific
pat on the back. They too have flown.

Surprise at absence snares us like a web.
The shops are suddenly stuffed with specimens

 – fresh from attics – and animal poems top
the best-seller list. "Come back," we want to say,

"with your hoof or paw, webbed-foot, claw;
or let the hairy legs of the huntsman spider,

in the dead of night, caress our faces
as once we feared they might, assisting screams

of turbulent love – for this extremity
is worse by far, our eyes blind as bullets

now no creatures arrest our sight."
Here's dislocation: a world comprising faces

yoked to office, street or parking lot
where neither bird nor insect fly

and furnish mystery. For company, exposure
to our shadows. Bones. Or dreams of zoos

from which all creatures, astounded to be free,
leave tracks so shiny they guide each dreamer home.

PENCILS

1

I celebrate and sharpen
that masterstroke,
the pencil. Its touch

is firm but not final,
subtle foreplay
across the page

toward liberties
of print; and gentler
than a pen. Poised.

Blunt, near a rubber,
on my desk. Unless
it gets lost, another

one in a billion
with all its retractable
words yet to come.

2

Brilliance, mostly,
of length and width
at 45°: pressure

of habit connects it.
I write "such keen
engineering

receives scarce heed"
with this newly bought
shiny Staedtler HB.

3

My Spirax notebooks
agree – these descendants
from the original

Borrowdale graphite
models (cedar-cased)
are all the stationery

I need to keep
up to date. Line
breathing into line

down the page,
champion the heart
minute by minute;

chart regions
familiar and remote.
Ah, it's great

the way pencils brave
gales, or emotion,
and remain unbroken.

from The Islanders (2002)
and The Lives and Times of the
Islanders (2009)

VOLCANIC

Islands: the actively volcanic,
smoke signals centring sky and ocean.
Know them by their tongues of magma.

Cut to this island, cooled, its people,
books they pour out,
soft or hard cover, slim or fat,

printers hard at it way past midnight.
Words overflowing. Genres boil and bake,
and settle, ultimately, on what?

In a line, upon the island.
No escaping the words it generates –
they smoke out cats and ignite curtains.

The rumblings are frequent, wide and deep.
People's, not the island's. It's past
having any significant seizure.

LINEAGE

Let's say in the shadow
of a sea eagle
a sailing ship dropped anchor.

What the crewman possessed,
eyeing the starveling port
from the deck,

counted for less than a whisper
in a brawling bar,

the name recorded, nevertheless,
in court records
for petty theft.

None of this is true.
He simply changed his identity
and lied his way
into another story

and rivers parted
as, on horseback, he advanced
his good fortune.

Word has it, his true love
was aristocratic with a gift
for clairvoyance.

But who's kidding whom.
Now descendants hear versions
various as clues

or, to give their name
its due, trespass
on a credible truth.

OFF THE MAP

When in a glossy promotion
of coastline, the island
was simply left off

the residents reached
the conclusion they're an
expendable rock.

There were letters in the paper,
press releases, speeches,
possibly a forlorn
flag at half-mast.

Identity deleted,
close to the Continent,
who wouldn't make a fuss?
There have been wars for less

and more speeches.
It was unreal.

Something had to be done
on the cartographic front,
with allied strategic
representative missives

to give the people a respectable
presence among the tourist
brochures and logos.

So it happened, the absence
was flagged.
          News of this island:
bolshy inhabitants, often mad.

CONNECTIONS

1

To the top of the guest list
at Tourism's Annual Improver Prize
for Morphogenic Smiles,

and at other lavish events,

ascend the members
of well connected families
who in feuding groups
fall upon the booze.

2

On stubborn doors, in high places,
the aristocrats maintain
pneumatic pressure.

There is widespread tension
about the economic momentum
required to slam the doors back on them.

3

A neutral observer's voice
appeals for calm; that meddler,
quite frankly, should know better.

4

Then there is that unseemly debate
in a small auditorium
about the influence,

wide or newly weak,
of the old school tie.

The skies zigzag with lightning.

After an electrical fault is fixed
there's a split linked
to whether a patterned
or plain tie looks best.

FIREWORKS

A display is never
more than a few days away –

smoke and explosions at sundown
ricochet out to sea;

every creature flees the victory
of a football team, and holy events
are God's headache.

It's like flak minus
enemy attack.

Ah, but consider the attendant
echoes of this posture, out of sight,
in little factories,

the boom in a basement,
the dissonant windows,

talk in the squares, weeks later,
of body parts that went.

OLD WOMAN IN AN ANCESTRAL MANSION

Afternoon shadows are claws
hauling me back when, on the terrace,
I sit and resist. The sea's
unfettered, a shining blade
now I'm indoors, my mind
a drowning site for voices, wide
enough for rooms to prove
a perfect fit. Mirrors moon
over wrack of conflicts. The split
restless joint a parting gift;
a trick the generations
have played on me if the sum
of their endeavours, brave
as seafarers', is made complete
in the identity of an old woman
whose womb blanked out
what they began. I sever them
like a blade they'd grab.
I suck our name like a retreating tide.
The house is stranded, monument
to accretive reef-like dreams
I, the survivor, cannot leave,
salt in my hair, skin dry as weed.
My trick: to have made this place
so true to me its space adapts
understandingly – a wide-view mansion
which, overlooking ocean, traps.

A DEATH

A distant gunshot, then another,
quoting the horizons.

Years later, absence doubled
and redoubled: swelling of print.

Is the creature now extinct?
There are bones, evidence of a grin
and incapable wings.

It made a sound like a toad on heat
and won't, even now, let
the islanders alone –

has status, fame,
in keeping children with stories of it
at bedtime, awake.

This is resurrection
and revenge: lies and fabulous rumour
fuel its appetite;

brighten its eyes,
when they open,
yellow and black, piercing

oh, just to focus in the dark,
tenderly, tenderly, on offspring,

or else to scout, exaltant,
its bloody narrative.

A FIREWORK MAKER ON THE DOMESTIC FRONT

I try quietness, am a squib
at home; sea views. Arguments between
the wife and me peter out. She fumes.
The kids stand back and watch us
like an event. Volatile. She says
St. Catherine's martyrdom was nothing
to hers, and wheels around me as if
I'm hub of her favourite firework.
It's not just the saltpetre
on my clothes that follows me home.
I hold back, damp, in the know.
Protect my wick, if necessary.
Blast you, she says. If only.
Then at dusk, gunpowder light,
I'm gone to ignite the sky with salvos
for some celebration. Remotely.
A clifftop or field as if I'm sixteen
with guilt as large as other blokes'
shadows. I take charge of all
I know: the taper, flame. Sit tight.
The seconds tick. Till I shout, Go!
Now rockets are shrieking
toward the stars or, if not, I explode.

NAME OF THE ISLAND

Brisk traveller, antenna to antenna,
over mountain and river, echo
in some historic chamber
or else chiselled in stone
its letters line up like actors. Script also,
overnight graffiti; shapeshifter
attached equally to suitcases
and land – meaning coastline
emboldens it, except on a map.
Like gastropods, adjectives
batten on, weather words, maritime.
Then it's a beam from a lighthouse,
far off, now close to reefs, cliffs.
Watch out! Two syllables,
no three, relayed as the name
of the island – while wind screams
in rigging – prove, tales told,
to give the buoyancy needed.

BETWEEN THE ESTABLISHMENT

A fence, inspected, for frontline
of a feud; families
slammed like shutters
against ancient grudge.
Then a bird of passage,
town legend has it,
flapped idly back and forth
between bitter estates,
between splendid chimneys.
Weird contact, messenger
with a long cry like a valley
and, surely, partisan,
though neither side, spooked,
would claim its black shadow
or any fair perspective
about what it forebode
other than a share, in its beak,
of the abundant fieldmice.
They awaited developments
like old age, intermarriage.
Freaked by a bird, they were
respectful of limits.
There was no ready escape
across grey churning sea.
Until both sides saw
the real position this queer
bird prized was more akin
to a fence primed for sitting on –
and in opposition, telescopically,
a couple of bullets
dared agree on one thing.

HIGH VIEWS OF THE DEPARTMENT HEAD

Daybreak, I take Shovel, my dog,
for a walk. Miniature, island pedigree.
I named him for his excavations.
I protest. Then I'm shifting gears
as I glide toward the office;
tame my hair, on arrival, in the lift.
It shudders upward, multi-storey, to where
windows host promotional views like ads
right to the coast. High hopes.
A boost to the emblem that I chose:
a golden goose. No matter whether
the Department shrinks or grows,
it's boldly illuminated on the roof.
I close my door and walk
the mobile I know will ring:
money talks and, in translation,
so does a delegation. Suave
and remote, I fill their glasses.
I play it cool. I say, You want the views?
and fetch the ice. One or two?
Now in their estimation I rocket,
moon-walker, in the brilliant
glare of their attention. Ten million bucks
plus offers gets me there. RECOMMENDED
I stamp on their plans. Development –
highrise, golden eggs widespread
which in my position I neither file
nor duplicate nor, ever, confess refreshes
on close inspection, telescopic,
regulations for some rowboat shed.

SHOOTING SEASON

Swifts, sea eagles, a falcon
yet to dwindle to a fleck
in a telescopic sight,
are focus, near the coast,

of the shooters'
seasonal, diminishing
cocky pride.

Or else the mechanical
salutes of barrels infer
the men are fearful
beneath wide sky.

Now they're spread out
across the island
when, as usual, two skive off,
unshaven, shabby,
along a clifftop –
trigger-happy as remnants
of some wrecked platoon.

A pair of bloody losers,
the tourists jeered,
who in flight from postcard views
lose their hats. Nearby,
their four-wheel drive.

Five foreign hats for shooting practice
in lieu of birds,
and on the rocky ground
plastic cartridges,
an evacuated mound.

A dozen more to spiral
a swift's summer visit
into a reddened sea.

So many generations make this
a fait accompli.

Then there are roadsigns,
stunned letters in a village name;
garden gnomes on guard
at home, outstaring, late

a final outsized bullet.

HER SHOPPING LIST

bread and cheese
sweets
a lemon squeezer
magazines
soap
note paper
a pencil
a length of rope
ale
a fairy tale
hope
a telescope
some nails
a mobile phone
a cure for vertigo
a seaside home
a key
freedom
ticket for a boat
fruit in season
biscuits
bags of crisps
bliss
a man
a prince
who can
remember
a list

WIFE OF A SHOOTER

At last he's gone with the gun,
handling the barrel as if it's alive
after long winter, limp, in the cupboard.

My release. This is his season,
he thinks. I flirt in front of TV;
buy a new skirt, unnoticed, in the shadow

of migrating birds. My tricks
are not hit or miss. Wingbeats
overhead and he's alert. Bang! Bang!

The echoes, youthful, I recollect.
We knew the hillsides, getting the hang
of his release. Unshaven, frisky,

he's at home out there, aiming high;
his blindness lifts for a twitching wing.
Cruel migration – the kids saw how mercy

skirts long oiling of a single bore.
Muzzled words. Now flight primes me:
he'd notice first, on a bird, its ring.

ELEGY FOR A DOG

Loyal dog, you obeyed one last
command and, still lying there, hours later,
gave us a clue to your condition.
Throughout the island bells rang out
– it being Sunday – and somewhere
fireworks ignited sky. A blessing.
Now other dogs, as small as you,
will be terrified by human antics.
Not the least, let's now admit it,
by shoes poised to kick and more than bruise.
It was, they said, your bloody yap.
More likely that your courage
in the face of threats, our neighbours',
was inversely related to your size
– a rat comes to mind – and inspired
an insurgent lust to silence
a larger mutt. Thankfully, it was our fond
command that did the trick.
So, with this send-off, the attraction
of your breed escapes the neighbours.
Let no-one talk of a replacement.

OUT OF THE PICTURE

Formal folk in rows, buttoned-up,
earnest, hours to firm creases and pleats –
a group photo made
when photos were slow.

Two faces, an immediate blur;
a tree, in the background,
the island's botanical signature.

Perhaps someone, gap-sized,
had fled for a prolonged piss;
and prominent noses
suggest a surge of relatives.

It's a guess that no-one
could suss the man in the cocked hat
at the back – plain shady

on a clear day the photographer read
for shadows and depth.

Let's not forget him,
reliable, nameless magician in his darkroom,
group reassembling, on command,
in a sharp-smelling developer bath.

Then soon they had nothing
further to do, outside the picture,
but unbutton their fronts,
kick off their shoes;

anonymous enough, again,
in the raw, or cold in freak rain,

to care a jot for the questions
yet – distant, so much later –
casually to be shaped:

who are these people? Where?

from Speed & Other Liberties (2008)

THE SUNLIGHT INLAND

1

After days of mean drizzle, low cloud
like a used rag smearing the windows, to go
out into sunlight is free refreshment,
a border crossing, one front step down,
clothes like sheaths loosening for skin
to bud on the streets. Sills with their flowerpots, gates ajar,
the buildings have arrived here, row after row,
so absorbed by the light no hinge gives an inch
to the longest shadow, the century that measured them.

Unless money, superabundant, illuminates
age to a developer, their persistence shines.
The length of the High Street bold graffiti extrapolates.
Balconies are like smallholdings to some families.

In an instant, light rinses and dries pale strollers –
through the parks, litter again, as if shaken out, stale.

Speeding clear of the coast, it's still hours
till the neighbour, the stubborn one, will ease
the car into a space on the street he sees freshly as his.

2

The congestion, the accident, rink rage,
and then, in the rear, the skater
trained in the tropics, St Moritz in the sun ...

Ice in the right latitude,
the gun. He could reckon the Olympian
thighs of the pack, their speed leaning
into the Utah arena, before he left Queensland.
The deep chill of their streets; steam breath.
And surely this: he could hazard their grace.

From the line where, for the gold, the skaters
got set, ready and went, each could freeze
his ambition with a glance, the lad
who'd brought charm like his sunlight
inland to the Winter Olympics,
slow in their wake and, as surely,

handily placed as their skates
shaved fresh ice, the crowd pressing
forward to the edge of the rink.
He just had to wait. No one could blame
liquefaction – his tropical gaze –
for the collapse of the pack a long
second ahead of him, the derangement of legs,

and how he flew past them, and won.
The sunlight somehow redeemed him, in any case.

3

Geraniums, close to doorways, survive night air.
Monsteras, frangipani on a terrace
might be invited to impress; early guests
when frost withdraws unfashionable
influence towards its north polar address.

Where canapés and fizz are mixed,
there's a taste for the tropics –
sunlight far-reaching across the continent.
A longing in gardens
for African heat on soft skin
like a text, evolutionist, its covers
unopened since autumn –

and for water, embryos' world
amid wealth, distant as the coast, yachts
anchored in harbours for the annual return.

The plants in privileged settings
thrive on attention, and get it.
Where they originated, the hotels,
the touts, and tours are ready.

4

Late afternoon, the days' warmth stored
in brickwork, a lone round-the-world yachtsman
writes for posterity about a landlocked country –
how as an overland traveller in Africa
he conjured for a woman, waves,
sheet lightning at night, turbulent
dark water then morning composure,
(after him, for others recurrently, he thought,
this being as close as we get to eternity).

In her hand, a creased photo of ocean.
One good eye to follow his longing
beyond rickety buildings, ruined hills
and the hum, under clear sky, of impending heat.

Her sea words, rapt immersion, in afternoon sun.

This sailor's escape – weeks inland to the west,
and to show for it, photos,
village close-ups of her faraway look. His limits.
Immediate views of a withered harvest.

5

The pink slipstream of a southbound jet, like a graze.

Dawn arrives in towns with parcels of light, tossed,
window-size, into houses; transports the gardens –
ground moisture rising through leaves.

Late spring has delayed them. Europe wakes;
seeds, raked into rows, germinate.

The warm length of the country, trippers'
cameras range against nature, detain
fugitive sun, deeply inland, out in the open.

Each vantage, foreground,
angle, an intake of breath

ninety-three million miles, and a car ride,
from the source, at last, of the fun.
Glossy prints showing off, days later,
how far into the heat-haze they'd gone.

THE MORNING OF THE FUNERAL

The Saturday newspaper, front page scanned,
he'll spread out liberally on the table later.
Right now, the washing-up with last night's
pasta sauce smears must be done; the hot water
fogging his reading glasses which he folds.
The wide kitchen window is a suitable height
for him but not his early-risen wife. Ajar, the garden gate.
Plates in the dishrack gleam white, lily white,
and he realises, suddenly, pausing, fork in hand,
he's not seen that so many lemons
have appeared this year on the hardy tree
as if some citizen has flipped a switch,
bright yellow citrus globes among
the deep perennial green. A blackbird
stretches, like gum, a worm. A knife
as sharp as the one he slowly wipes
might have a price – and now the rack is laden.
He checks the clock. If he doesn't iron a shirt
and go – some years since he's seen her –
he'll kick around the house, glance
at one or another mirror, and see
in so doing this would come at a greater cost
than resolution to pay last respects, poised
as he now is with a sharpened sense
of choice between two acts of hard self-interest.
He pulls the plug. The bird has won
its tug-of-war and flown. On the window, he notices
what's left of his concentration is his breath.

POEM FOR THE REFUGEES

Not a position any would say they'd die for,
though shadowy movements might require

a leg up or a ladder's final rung.
The office with bright credentials, sun,

inherited shop or a backstreet house,
quickly banished since like migrant birds

they flee over waterless land and crave
status higher than the hasty graves,

lower than an exchange of bullets.
Whatever they dream about or expect

will long outlast reports that trace
groups camped near coastland, on their way

to spook night rooms lit by TVs –
nurses, cooks, someone's cousin with a degree.

NIKE AT THE MEGALITHS

At the megalithic temple
in early afternoon heat
a sunscreened woman walks away
from her tour group, the tone

of the amplified commentary
slick as instructions to youths
on a sports field till,
at the perimeter, close to olive trees,

it's a slight irritation
like the last blowfly in a house
where for a reader her book
is a passport into immersion.

There, near the huge stones,
where to the right she can see
the continuous present
of the blue Mediterranean

it seems a small step
through light reflected off limestone
to see robed priests and linger
as if in 4,000 B.C. in the heat

of a primitive cosmology.
The clay women, swollen as loaves,
in their alcoves. Puzzle
of blood in the dust. What's known

of their rites? Her guesswork.
The woman like an ad for Nike,
slim, blonde, American,
has only minutes to be amazed

like an archaeologist who turns silent
in the presence of cave paintings
when, in torchlight, the active
figures somehow mirror him.

The arrangement of quarried stones
in the glare look to her
not like a ruin but seem
hoisted up, all of a sudden,

from the limescape. Dwarfed
she vaguely hears, again,
stray words from the megaphones
fade in and out, French then German,

wide of any cultural imagination
she's entranced by at Ggantija
as freshly as the sweat making
her bright summer clothes cling.

To return, like the caver, to the present
is a trek via the Enlightenment
through the many ages of humankind.
Her Nike runners are fit for it.

The sea shimmers and glints there,
a tabula rasa. She's recomposing,
with effort, her febrile life on the fringe
of the tour group, modernity

— the megaliths a gang of shadows, lost
cosmology protected from the olives —
when, as if conjured, a silent jet
splits the sky overhead, like a zip.

MR HABITAT'S HOME POLICY

Insurance? I don't need it. How many times
has this house burned down? It requires no fingers.
Candles, flaming toast, illuminate its persistence.
Thieves lurk like a virus. The neighbours
are sickened by nicked equipment.
I'm immune: airy cupboards, Spartan rooms.
I go on tour. Acoustic. My song and dance
electrifies the wide-eyed passers-by.
A hail of coins, I'd like; a trickle makes me fitter.
I'm a survivor, made to last, a fifties radiator.
It figures: assessments freak at former houses,
trashed or incinerated. Have I made claims!
The premiums went through the roof like flames.
Now the odds agree, I've exhausted probability.
My new policy: full risk. No exclusions. Wars.
Sonic booms. Riots. Lightning. I'm clearly safe.
But I keep the photo albums handy, just in case.

THE OXFORD ENGLISH DICTIONARY

The fruitful relationship
between his biceps and dictionary,
lungs and literary adventuring

– in and out of classy bookshops,
top end of town – faltered
with the twenty volume Oxford

he insisted on shifting to his shed
in a single go. The man's past forty,
and, sure, he can flex

a good vocabulary. But this ...
At home, sun-blinds,
which he calls awnings, down.

The dog, with some polysyllabic
appellation, nearby. Subtract
the vocabulary of his hectic

explanation and, on the path,
he might with one book fewer
have had a chance. The neighbours

don't resist great onomatopoeia
when, as it's made, they hear it.
They have spine. His, stuffed (he says),

compels him to retrace his run
through fifty classics plus bedside Roget,
pausing, only now, for lighter fiction.

CRIME FICTION

The suburb was cocksure recent, professional
class, double-brick houses, mid-height
eucalypts along the Beaumaris nature strips;
each garage emptied of a Ford or Holden

on day release up to the smoke.
Monday. The coarse yodels
of magpies announced one yard or another
along grid-like streets seized

by the Americana of a developer.
At 16 Florida, a breeze
off Port Phillip Bay frisked
the native ti-trees and stoic camellias.

The ding-dong doorbell announced the cop.
His hat was off when, around eleven
it was my turn to sing in the study.
He commanded the desk. I had my story ready.

Pen in hand, his eyes were steady.
The stuff he wrote, questions, answers,
formed part of my inquiry
when, like Chandler's Marlowe, I risked

a certain involvement in this case.
For the cop, it was pretty much open and shut,
on the previous day, the doctor gone, my mother's
body sent to the morgue, a duty done.

I had to become a tough dick for this,
or fake it. Adopt a style,
just to get by. For a flying start,
see off a wet tell-tale pommy manner.

What did that big-jowled Aussie cop
— methodical, slow — make of father and son
glossing a loss, right from under their noses,
in proper far-off London diction?

He was no dope. I reckon he thought,
crazy English, in a new abode. The whys
and wherefores of the crime became no clearer
when father's pipe smoke filled the room.

Mother had once been found, in the garden, prone.
Finding her in bed, colour gone, was for me
no afternoon bed of roses, I didn't say, schooled
— smooth of face — to be formal, courteous.

Now the cop had ammo for the inquest,
complete with suicide note and empty brown
bottle of barbiturates. He vamoosed.
There was, I puzzled, more to this case.

Scotch whisky, a madhouse, an outer
London district, as it surfaced. I needed dosh,
dough, lolly, a swag of loot, and the years to grow
tall enough to stash it. To get close.

I almost whizzed past our old manor.
This was a trajectory that, slow at first,
had, gaining evidence, gathered pace.
I confess, officer, my driving's dangerous ...

Luckily, the filth were on the beat
or chasing crims. 184 Joel Street,
two storey, semi-detached, had shrunk like the economy
from its commanding, parental height,

to drab Middlesex real estate. In need of paint.
Opposite, the farm, once huge, had dwindled
inside its fences, and each oak tree with it.
It seemed a trick. I had to get the measure of this.

A neighbour said, "I last saw your mother
at the shops." Briefly, it seemed
she wasn't gone. Or furtive tears. I was after truth,
one that made things too rough, cast

her act as triumph over family tattle,
and all I was getting was a bad case
of displacement. Like Marlowe, I craved a drink.
An ominous flock of starlings swerved overhead.

Birds were the connection I really needed. Clues.
Blue tits, great tits, thrushes, wrens and robins
preserved in *The Observer's Book of Birds* and,
in our garden, safe from the slingshots of the farm lads. Mates.

Nippers. Shavers. In its cage our brisk canary
hopped, obsessed, from rung to rung;
clung to its bars, and twitched its head,
flitted from one side to another – stopped

to sing its domestic song. My mother hoovered,
cooked and scrubbed. I now saw the steps
she'd washed and swept. The tears and screaming
at a neighbour, while I hid under a polished table,

her version of the *Housewife's Blues*.
Played out by six o'clock, a brassy knock
announced her husband, and on her cheek
she got a peck. With this image I'd had enough

flashback – hit the road in my Morris Traveller,
took a slug of what I needed, and
the local roundabout more than once.
Headed to some place with some kind of future.

There, via the highways of the sky, a span of birthdays,
rosellas hurtled from gum to gum tree,
made a lively racket above the latest
bayside houses that sheltered new retirees

and holidaying huntsman spiders. Leafy
Mount Eliza. Once an escape, now a capitulation.
On my own good authority, I knew
my mother's memory was captive here in Unit 1,

curtains half drawn, windows shut
and there, once again, I wasn't about
to let a smokescreen put me off.
My father lit his pipe. I poured the Scotch.

The land of opportunity was, across the table,
a shaft of light, and I wanted more
than pat expressions like "sick", "depressed",
the slammed door of the madhouse where

gradually she'd knitted bootees
and baby vests for me, a swell, peripatetic
among the relatives. He was no snitch.
I had my father fingered but he was quick

to miss the real content of the Scotch whisky.
The light was gone, and the drink to release
the sort of light I wanted. Each time we parted company,
our accents had long since already done it.

Marlowe, be my guide out of the quiet streets
tough vernacular has failed to reach ...
It was daylight when, with a handshake,
I was off again. On whom or what

to pin the guilt was like trying to wrench
an oyster open with a stake
from a picket fence. In Mount Eliza, I knocked
a few about in passing with my desert boots

as if that machismo could be a swift
rehearsal in getting some villain to blab,
spill the beans, fess up, or sing some kind of truth
about this hush-hush bit of mother trouble.

I wasn't done with yet. She deserved a better press
than some thin notice in the Births and Deaths,
and being somewhere between both myself,
felt I owed it to her. There were the relatives,

those she'd missed, whose aerogrammes
still slipped through the slot at manned chez Sant,
with the garish ads. For them to blab would need a catalyst.
Gentle persuasion. A prod. A spur. A sop.

Grief: compulsory re-runs from the sixties
of *The Saint* where Roger Moore gets the lovely girl, always,
and the villains. Right now, this case was getting me
no halo, few suspects, and a lack of sleep.

The development came with a call, long distance,
"I'm sorry to have to inform you …"
Rain hit the window with its wintry fist
and I dodged, shocked to find the right reply

among the orthodox list of words
lingering in the classifieds. With "much loved"
and "missed" to see him off, my long-lived father
maintained long silence as his privilege.

I hit the phone myself. Sitting, lost for words,
in the chilly, white, windowless room
with his body stretched out beneath a sheet
had made me garrulous, need to shed

what? Tears! Equal to an absent weight
in some accordance with the theory of Archimedes.
I was soon back among the rosellas and picket fences.
The family photo albums, spread about the lounge,

I now cracked open like cement.
Inside, a suspicious lot in posh
Edwardian dress, who've smartly
robbed posterity of any stock of mirth

and are sternly standing firm.
If I needed cheer, I wasn't going to get it here.
Nor did my mother, by the looks.
She stood among them, all stiff as a row of books

containing in her folks' Esher or Palmer's Green,
adventures with the drink and novel length TB.
The girl had it tough. There were many
factors – and I was counting – but they didn't yet

add up to her solution. On
the Bible of my mother's God
she'd reckoned in her note would take
care of the little family she'd signed off,

I could have sworn there was more evidence
that needed air. Right then, He wasn't beyond
a personal slating, or the specious range of shots,
in the albums, of English beauty spots.

I had the urge to wrap things up, reach the sort
of resolution that drives crime fiction
or a car towards its destination –
headlong down motorways where the macadam

ends, not with a twist, but requires a necessary
deceleration. I'd bet Marlowe would get
the drift of this, though not the
points for frequent flying. They were increasing.

The car squeezed smooth as toothpaste
between high hedges, hiding barley, along the lanes.
TV aerials, pert as rabbits ears,
were, on thatched roofs, the only evidence

of speed round here – except the flight,
from the smoke, of polite aunts and uncles
for their skirmish with the reaper.
In the windscreen, Devon dawdled

and Somerset slept. I accelerated,
with fresh dirt on the case, from those ancients,
towards a rough house pub I knew
to slug it out, scrap or scuffle

with a spectre. The joint was full
of ugly customers. I joined a shout.
On the walls enough stained memorabilia,
through the smog, to weigh heavily

on any sod's misplaced levity.
I grabbed my father and knocked him out.
Checked my knuckles, smiled, downed
a pint, and swore in chorus

with the aunts and uncles that when
the troubles began, had he been more willing,
less chilly … They'd blabbed. No grief
as catalyst from the sixties needed.

Just his absence, and a gentle nudge.
But six pints later, he was back, an unbloodied
spectre, for his own defence, and I was glad
he had a strong attacking right hook in him.

He'd got a slagging, and duly didn't want
to take a rap based on the angle
that being spliced was something he couldn't handle.
I staggered. Late, the pub was emptying. The bastards

couldn't see what the sodding fuss was all about.
None was a reader, yet each seemed
to turn, like a blurry page, and vanish
from this bit of action. I saw the way out

might be via another crazy institution,
now I'd got the lowdown on its whereabouts.
I needed to be sober – was closing in
on the next sinner that needed sizing up.

I looked at myself in the rear-vision mirror.
My features were less tired and ragged
after a week spent on the wagon.
I gulped some air. The car I left

at the mercy of the local tea leafs. A red Fiesta.
The secured, four storey austerity of the bin
looked in the drizzle like a prison.
Through the iron gates, I ventured

into Bedlam's Georgian next of kin – the breeze
frisking water off the winter trees –
glad to be too late by a century plus
to join the sightseers of the barking mad,

though I had no trouble letting loose
images of leglocks, the purge and the douche.
I sleuthed about where paupers once
had shaven heads and, later on, coves

sported Wilkie Collins beards; wanted out
of the restraints and handcuffs gripping
the Hanwell Asylum atmosphere.
Even after a quick escape to the modern

spin of varied tucker, open gate
and central heating, this seemed a curious refuge
for a new mother. I had the dirt on these places.
They breed foul language. She already had enough

to cope with – me, competing voices released,
post-natal, inside her head, and long before
TV crims got to tranquilise
many a fine expletive. It was quiet.

I sized up the silent, hunkered chapel
where, near the pulpit, the numbered hymns
were *All Things Bright and Beautiful*
and *The Lord is My Shepherd*. Outside,

I'd heard, on a light branch, high above,
a wet thrush sing. The fuckers, all, I could've
cried, convulsed her with electric shocks!
It would have resounded nicely in the cold

uncomprehending chapel. In my head,
the language of her medical records lingered
in busy polysyllables – the one fifties throng
scot-free of stigma. I snuck out through a side door,

a guilty party, took my loyal reflection
for a last stroll among the sudden puddles.
The guy who looked back up at me, windswept,
looked like trouble. I had him sussed –

flawed like all the rest. Cagey. The red Fiesta
remained unnicked. Soon I was flat out, first gear,
not looking back in thick outer London traffic, a Brunel
viaduct, off to my left, heading somewhere.

THE LEMON TREE AT 42° SOUTH FROM 52° NORTH

Whether or not it's fruiting
I want to know – have sent a spy
to check, brown eyes
above the back fence, if the tenants are in.
I planted it but the lemons
– if there are any – tang their tea
or fish fresh off the boats from the Southern Ocean.
They're welcome to them but had better
look after the young tree that would benefit,
in warm privacy, from a jet of piss.
I say this from a long way off, far
north of lands in which citrus fruits flourish,
and so my thoughts, under grey skies, ripen
with the desire to revisit Sicily
where bright citrus and crime
get along nicely.
It's a matter of degrees. Not even the Gulf Stream
can force its influence to favour, here,
a backyard lemon tree
like mine, and like me
a sun lover – tough as rind
in my no latitude gangster shades.
Yes, the tree had better be in good shape.
Bad luck I'll not be attacked
by homesickness, a test
many others are felled by, certain
where home is, like a clan –
for me, rootless, even the promise
of fresh lemons (with honey) can't induce it.
The tree, I hope, is tough as boots,
bred to weather a brutal landlord, any bitter
tenants squeezed for cash –
and in my own time, a surprise,
I'll show up and handle, easily, any fruit.

JASMINE IN A TEMPLE GARDEN

At a sunlit Taoist temple, in jasmine scented air,
I consort with a stranger to Edwardian
suburban gardens, yet then to make a fashionable entry;

arrived here by inking a street map
onto the back of my hand, in the way tough guys
seek reassurance by having tattoos pricked

onto their mountainous biceps –
wish, when the post arrives from "home",
I felt suddenly homesick to get a quick

whiff of the gravitational certainty
that shows where such a place is, in the way
migratory birds and postmen know.

When the exotic perfumes strewn by the Chinese
floral diaspora – jasmine, daphne, buddleia –
first made a summer in the west, this scene was set.

EXPOSURE

At the instant of exposure
film bespeaks a printed
place and its name, in my camera.
Pocket-size, close sidekick,
it travels with me, and the blank
spools, metaphors for journeys
about to be taken, where
shadows of pagodas wheel
west to east, or a train is hunched
at dusk in a station –
focal points for all the local
possibilities of light that,
in any case, dissipates.
                        A shadow
since I leave no print,
I'm visitant recorder
of cooking smells in walled Pingyao
or, further north in Shanxi, hear
the thud of the pick a peasant
swings to shift the earth he needs
to till, for bricks. A learner,
in a land of records, checks,
the character for China looms on signs,
freewheeling caption on my films

winding and rewinding, north to south;
and there will be evidence
of spring light on jagged mountains,
multi dishes at a table
set for six, against so many odds
for such exposure. The films say,
just believe it! Not in a fix
like their chancy taker, questioning,
behind the seasoned camera,
the drive to record such sights –
its shutter, as if mistrustful,
in a rush to seize and verify.

PHOTOGRAPHS OF SHANDONG PEASANT CHILDREN
for Hu Min, photographer

Did these children, resolute or grinning, want to visit
the city? So many with an intent way of looking
at the viewers their photographer breeds. T-shirts,
pants like westerners', duplicated, they're ready

to hit the streets of the rumoured masses. One, it's pictured,
at a time. I'd like to give them a hand:
cash, more bottom drawer clothes, or patronage
in another out of place form. But here, quickly,

their identities have grown, the mischievous posers.
That's a lot of land to defend with a single toy gun,
right across the stubble to the horizon –
reason enough for him to stay put. The rare key dangling

from another's belt, boldly, might have uses anywhere.
Not for this master the limits of a heated bedroom.
Who in this meeting of many gets the measure of whom?
Their eyes follow me closely down the expressway home.

TWO WAYS OF LOOKING AT LANDSCAPE

1

(China)

Not for us Li Bai's sublime moon, his uplifted eyes;
the terrain is steep, and Chinese herbs
I'm shown are prepared to save us, by degrees,

from sore feet and vertiginous thoughts.
Put a lyric in the pot and it would produce steam.
We take each step wisely and, later, tea.

2

(Sweden)

Two of us here with words to share. This northern landscape
echoes them: fir, *furn*; birch, *bjork;* lily, *lilje*.
The *snegle* I nearly crush, and the *orm*.

Up ahead our related words are gathered, damp, darkening,
till we'll not notice the forest for the words.
They'll be the light we guess by. We'll see.

ATTITUDES IN A POSSIBLE FOOD MUSEUM

In the food museum – breakfast room – a wish
that the tired toast and jam didn't show their origins
in polystyrene and resin; and the poached eggs,
which might resist a fork, looked runny.
Worldwide cuisine, as the sun shines,
is ready to be served: barritos, muesli, crepes.
Not as filling as nasi goreng released
from a mould to make an authentic
habit of inhabiting space. Find the right
button to push (the attendant's on hand)
and there's the distracting whiff of egg foo yung.
For the kids, more interaction: washing-up liquid
and a sink choked with filthy dishes.
Nearby, a slice of bacon – streaky – reveals
little of a massive sow, but provides
sufficient evidence to show she's missing.
For all of Africa, a sack of flour.
Someone's crying. Real, or another display?
The attendant, weary-eyed and sour, adds
his quota of animation. There's a fan.
He watches the food of ancient Egypt, Japan.
All the long day it's 8 a.m. He'd like a break
from the routine ways the world gets fuelled.
By the stopped clock, daily, his urge for haste.

HEAT AND LIGHT

The question is, did she lose sight
of him or vice versa when, one afternoon,
crickets in the incendiary forest split
seconds into ticking thousandths,
gully to dry gully, the day decompressing ...

A cracked window pane, back home,
a fragmented view of watered lawn –
the landlord, bossed by cause and effect,
not convinced their screamed invective
was the culprit, the heat intense.

Eventually, he lost sight of her, electric
in a red silk dress, at the airport;
glass doors closing on the hubbub.
She watched intently, relieved
to see his plane puncture the bluest sky.

VOICE THEORY AND PRACTICE

Words did him in, a few or many,
or so I heard, the way he spoke them
got on her nerves. His hygiene
she could like, even his CDs
but not nowadays his speech –
wished she'd been worded up
last century about the importance
of an appealing voice.
Even in bed he sounded like a turd.
Or so I heard, at length
and at a pitch that would have been considerate
if I were deaf. This said something
about his hearing, though I hadn't heard
he's losing it, but now I knew.
I wanted to get a few words in,
think she didn't like the sound
of my voice either
and therefore see me, breathing,
as any desirable part of her future.
I made no comment. In the cafe
everyone now had significantly turned up their voices
as if amid a revolution –
an epidemic from which, happily,
I remained immune, though in cahoots
with the source of the infection.
For the record, her ex-man,
in my view, doesn't sound too bad
unless he sings, but that's not the issue,
speech is, its necessary caress, the theory
of its significance in relationships –
and the pandemonium that ensues
when the accused is hanged
on any verbal avenue of his own defence.

MR HABITAT AND THE PROTECTION RACKET

Out of the house, I take books for protection.
Pricey. On buses, trains – in cafes –
they save me from dangers. Every page.
I glance up, lower my reading glasses,
see how many others are dependent
on hefty novels or self helps with bold covers.
A lot look pale. For this they pay,
scan the reviews, and cough up again.
What I shell out is my own business
but, sure as hell, it's not *The Book of Kells*
saves me, in heavy traffic or stymied
by a cancelled train, from old age.
A real page turner has got the force
to hold at bay the pricks who profit,
at increasing speed, from urban damage –
and it's a thriller if their regulators
know how but not when they're going to cop it.
I pay. I pay. There's sod all chance
this bout of spending will ever stop. Now the room
I call my study is full of muscle, wall
to wall. Shuttered. And where I tough it out.

LONG WAIT AT QUICK SHOE REPAIRS
on my birthday

On a small town sidestreet
between a tattooist and antiques,
Quick Shoe Repairs.
Lone customer at the counter,
I'm walker, traveller, loiterer,
as at a bar or hotel reception
awaiting service, the repairer
in well-worn overalls, at work,
though I can't see them, on shoes.
He's facing a machine, elbows busily
going in and out, a professional
runners', amid the hum.
For this, I've traversed the globe,
in planes, through puddles,
down starlit roads – my sweaty shoes
at the ready in hotel rooms
with *in case* of *fire*
instructions on the doors,
and am not alone: above the machine
and repairer's bent
concentrating head, shelves
of shoes, forever married
through thick and thin
– now packed in bags –
attest to the demands of distance.
There's the smell of rubber, glue
(homely enough in a home for shoes),
 a machine for stitching, and one
for stretching; also a bin,
hard to see, for the pairs
that don't make it through.
Right now, I can see
the repairer's doing his best
to resurrect shine, a well shod future,
and in this circumstance, unique,
I must wait, impressed by lank
shoelaces, black and brown, longing

on a wooden rail, to get a life;
or else check out cans of polish,
many brands, the merest smear
set to reflect this street's edge
on all other latitudes of light —
and so I, too, by my wristwatch,
soon, soon, will flee this limbo;
the repairer's doomed, firm
grip on transient matters, released
to hand me, gift-like, wrapped,
my newly soled and shining shoes.

SAXOPHONE IN A PAWNBROKER'S WINDOW

Lost days when cavernous notes
reverberated seismically into the night,
or rose like an exotic flower,
wild and potent, a soloist's territory
far from eyes locked
on the instrument's price.

The neighbours wished for him
and his gleaming saxophone, a gig,
or frozen keys, glad to miss
the magic of his fingertips.

Now it's a mirror for peering
shoppers, madly skewed;
and at a stretch along its tube,
the street curves weirdly
where the saxophonist
lost control of the one bright
ally with any value –
a beacon among cold rings
and trinkets for him to brave
the crazy way back
to meet his own reflection,
just in time, and get the music out.

EXCURSION, DELAYED
(Iceland)

Via the airy corridors that led to heated
senior school geography lessons, I have arrived
for the long excursion into a necessary land
where definitions find abundant form and substance.
The other pupils all have fled;
as has the fine teacher who, with his lisp,
sweated over "glacier" and "scree", then later quit.
Now, to the left, a frozen river of ice, a tongue
stuck in the escarpment valley, really moves
the eye from one formation to another –
Vatnajökull's névé field, a counter-
pressure in this region of tectonic shifts
where now and then the keen excursioner will stop
and expand his collection of igneous rocks.
The peaks of the volcanoes are in the clouds
and whatever rumblings happen in their craters
will happen for others, later. The wind is freezing.
Protection is afforded in the fjords
 – not confined, I now see, to coastal Norway –
though the fauna (e.g. eider ducks) ignore it.
Heat happens in the geothermal cracks and fissures
– *fumaroles* is the word I'm seeking – and the steam,
sulphurous, stinking, like rotten egg gas
makes it a relief not one class clown
is here to divert attention from a natural
function of this planet. Or stress, except perhaps
in passing, that in unfamiliar places
naïve curiosity is renewed – and a car, wrong
on the back home side of a road, is corrected quickly
travelling past fresh stretches of jagged magma.

TASMANIA

The state bearing a seafarer's name,
distant now, albatross range, from its link
with the polar continent – tectonic shift
small tremors communicate. Moored yachts
clink their rigging in bays. Skewed island,
all that mountainous weather-burdened weight in the west!
Shouldn't the sheltered east, with its vineyards and holidays,
be scolded for escaping the west's gales and rain,
the lit townships far out in a stormy night,
the straining forests, sea rage?
There's neither balance nor parity.
The real culprits have long since rumbled away
from where there's detritus of glaciers and awesome volcanoes.
But not icy air, sudden, hyping latitudes south
or from northern states, desert heat. Here,
pelicans and seals can choose their extreme.
Jetties wade into the sea, meantime, tentatively.
Each channel and bay with a European name,
just to repeat them is transporting
and then, for a while, History
– bloody, manacled, barbarous –
chides onlookers for taking pleasure
within its proximity like a squall
unsettling a glassy lake, and makes
imaginations take root or grow defiant as plover.
In the forests red waratahs open like claws;
bottle-brush flowers tally a hundred domestic chores.
High shine and danger combine in black snakes.
Around the coast and inland there may be species,
it's claimed, that elude being cited and named.

THE BANANA'S REPUBLIC

I vote for the banana, fruit of first choice
– before the lemon – in a
preferential system, and, hungry,
make it obvious on buses, trains
as do, between sets, sweaty
first class tennis players,
the abiding issue, for the fit,
being that the flesh is good for muscle tissue.
I vote for the serotonin
within it to defeat depression,
useful after some presidential elections;
and for me its shape, like a ready smile,
reveals a sunny disposition
which convinces, without lies or guile,
there's potassium to lessen my neighbour's
high blood pressure. I vote this the fruit
of first resort for its ample,
winning program and, a clincher,
its natural, efficient package.
I peel this pleaser, serious lunch, linked
to the rain and soil and forests, legislation,
north and south of the equator,
and to the urgent issue
of there being no bananas
left in the bowl on the table
or worse, in most of the world's grocers,
on parade under the banner
of Fair Trade – with a less delicious crop
this might disrupt a good digestion.
The sweet and creamy flavour
gets my vote – and as for the name's
Arabic derivation, *banan*, a finger,
it's a global index that points,
among the bright contenders, to the best.

ABUNDANCE

The captain of the boat, a handy man
without a crew, clearly knows of any dangers
while departing from Castle Haven, and soon he's taking
a zig-zag route along the jagged splendour
of the Atlantic coast, careful of the rock stacks
and buckled, rearing islands, till he sights
to starboard, the smooth emergence
in the moiling sea of a minke whale, and shouts.
For his dozen passengers, a brief appearance, thrilling,
before it dives and continues feeding,
as the boat resumes its jaunty route.
Till another appears as if to let the windswept
watchers know how tantalisingly little – a shiny back –
of its vast journey they will get to see,
the captain always on the lookout, with a cigarette
to aid his concentration. Easier to see,
recumbent on the rocky islands, is the colony
of piebald seals who share the luxury
of being released, albeit briefly,
from essential labour. They watch the watchers.
Shudder off the rocks, dive, and surface,
big-eyed, attentive to something odd.
The boat now so close the watchers can admire their whiskers.
What the seals see underwater, mackerel and herring,
is clear for them as for people watching a captive shoal
in a coastal resort's Underwater World. Today, the sea.
Gannets, from somewhere near the sun,
jack-knife into the water with a shocking impact
that must – imagine it – dazzle the fish into breaking
rank in all directions, like silvery splinters,
and the taciturn captain says
the birds snatch them on their fast ascent
back to the surface. It emerges slowly,
he once did have a crew and lived from fishing.
That's what the other seabirds, guillemots,
petrels, shearwaters are also doing now, full time,
large flocks drawn, as the boat is, to abundance

and, the well-thumbed bird books show, watchers'
love of linking with the many birds still here,
house martins, long before there were houses,
breeding in the cliffs – and the watchful puffins.
Imagine the terrible absence if all this was damaged.
There may be returns aplenty. The captain, alert eyes
on the sea, knife-bright, has lost nothing of his appetite.

from Fuel (2009)

REVISITING CLIFFS

Never too late
to whistle out the boy
in you, the one who is going to be the death
of both parents,
              scramble up
a wind-sculpted cliff face;
clamber left then right
to sidestep an overhang in a quest
to get at the fossils.
The sea sloshes
among the rocks at the bottom.

The next thing to avoid
is vertigo, of late a visitor
to heights, so
it's handy to relate
to the brave man
ventilating your name – and right now
at a stretch grips
a ledge – that the sedimentary layers
were, in the Jurassic, base
of the ocean

which puts quick
heartbeats into perspective
during the ascent
of rock that's risen
to the point of an afternoon
in thrall to deep curiosity
which is no height at all.

It's best to grip
this once-beneath-sea cliff,
hang on to the knowledge
that a phylum with a glimmer
in it of mammal swam there and ate,

and get giddy
with the wonder of it – the lengths to which legs
would go to get immersed
in needs beyond the reach of H_2O.

The cliff
has risen amidst a vast list
of extinctions, like the mass
of some palaeontological
gap the gulls curve
away from to continue their
delicious and still available
diet of *fruits de mer*.

What a strange wonder,
on this latest day of all creation,
to be human, scramble up
a cliff face to extract,
with a pick, a bunch of old stones

and look into it deeply for orientation.

MARVELLOUS HARBOURS

Picture this: a fishing boat, days out
on the ocean, makes an entrance, small
and free of sway, amid a suddenness of settlement.
What the harbour absorbs, routinely,
happens without fanfare. The sea
nuzzles a fleet, like animals asleep.
There is expectation and, always, a rapid passage
into marvellous harbours
as well as a vantage to photograph
the panorama, a diversion, under a clear sky,
from the good anchorage. In a mist, history
will report defences, batteries, forts
for the sake of prized interior water.
When the boats are captive, now
and foreseeably, the wind's storm-force.
Then the harbour discreetly
suffers its crazy creases, while the ocean,
madder, is tearing its clothes to pieces.
The harbour, you name it, each one
concentrated: Valletta (top of the list
for conflict), St John's, Halifax, Hobart ...
There it's always the limit, in high wind,
to upset a menu, à la carte,
and the general composure,
off the coast, of a luxury liner.
Everything needed right then to be
on its best behaviour: famished gulls,
buskers, drunks, a well-pressed
sheeny water. Better, as most do, more cheaply,
to arrive by air! Better get a grip ...
For this ship, wealthy foreigner,
there will be fanfare and possibly on deck
a band under shelter, and the mayor looking sunny.
It's best, if fish stocks are wrecked,
to fish tourists for money – only the panorama,
when it's visible, is sure to be without charge.
That's marvellous! And the streets like cordage

wrapped firmly around water and motion,
town driven by wind and the boats on petroleum –
the harbourmouth, wide or a devil,
to the wide world always open, spotted
first at sea quest and cannon level,
beating hollow the casual, elevated
pleasure of seeing all that has followed.

MR HABITAT'S OWN BONES

Crossed-legged in denim, I sit listening
though I'd rather be walking,
                                      re-visit the one
great nursery lesson, maybe head off for a drink.

Here, there are so many predatory chairs
sucking in victims like peppermints.
I ask, did we cope with the Bronze Age for this?
The crib? Or, once upon a time, the ocean?

All the geologic time and muscle
to get upright, find the right balance,
and someone important shows up
for a lecture and I'm listening attentively,
no question – spine, fibula, femur,
all the apparatus of *Homo erectus*,
present, representative, sedentary
even, and especially, the inner ear's
small ossicles.
                    No place in this soft tropic
to let the mind wander, get lost
in sportive primordial thought, falter there
and slip on brother slime –
no clever x-ray to thus locate
any break, even though, *raison d'être* of a chair,
bones are prepared to be far off
from here. Patella. Tibia. Tarsals.
In the marrow, deeply keen to get elsewhere.

DEDICATION TO A POTTER WASP

Allow me, this day and any other, the energy
and dedication of the potter wasp
which flies with pellets of clay
from the rainforest clearing to this verandah;
a loner who has built the cells for her nest on a sill
while I, sedated by tropical heat, watched.

For she has done this without let up,
constructed her adobe complex all week,
both worker and architect in one;
each cell like a reduced earthen vessel
from early civilisation, the wet clay
tamped into shape, by her antennae,
which in spite of the damp quickly dries.

Only when great rain isolates this house
– our view lost in cloud – and loudly hammers
the iron roof to prove, even at a distance,
there's a place at this height humans have made,
does she take a break. The male,
I've noticed from my recliner, is ever elsewhere
and, as far as assistance goes, fails.

Then she's back, busy in daylight, resting at night –
and how she must need that rest wherever
she goes for it within the forest where goannas,
half way up trees, seem to do little else,
and pythons thick as thighs doze
in their camouflage. She, in contrast, is brightly striped.

Yellow and black. Vampish. Tiny waist. Dangerous!
She stings and paralyses caterpillars as meat
for her future babies. I know this, from a distance
and keep it as, from her fine abdomen,
she deposits the eggs, stocks the larder,
and stoppers with clay each round entrance, like a bottle.

Nine cells I've greeted – two already set hard
when I arrived as a guest – each deftly erected
during slack afternoons or treks from the house;
the lot being rendered – this northern wasp cannot stop! –
smooth as a pot, while I, sluggish in the tropics, praise
this maker, now pack to fly in pursuit of the south.

THE HOUSEHOLD MOTH

The zoologist I quizzed
about a creature's life-span

said, "About three years," and then,
"It only has so many heartbeats."

That night I watched a moth
exhaust its vital store, amid

throbbing conversation and sullen chores.
There, on the carpet, wings

as if in prayer,
it reached its limit,

bank account, to the last cent,
withdrawn; no fuel

to keep the engine revving;
a quota of sun and moonshine

used not a second
too late or soon;

validity snipped;
camouflage lost;

all communication,
on schedule, broken off;

its chunk of time,
a preordained package deal

(no refunds) satisfactorily
run, accidents and mishaps

notwithstanding. The household,
numbed, ticked along without it.

THE MARRIAGE VOW

Each time we hit turbulence, it seems new –
a single crack and every dish is doomed.
If she leaves me, I'll say I'll leave her too.

When things are fine, the world is made for two
knives, forks and spoons, her crazy hound ungroomed.
I say I'll do it and I sometimes do.

I never balk at polish, brush and shoe,
though she's thought shoes of mine beside hers bloomed.
If she leaves me, I've thought I'll leave her too.

How little are the things that test the glue
of marriage. Cracks. Shoeshine. Socks. The car *varoomed*.
I thought I'd cool it but it's hard to do.

Then newly out of somewhere, like the flu,
there's strange reversal where alone I've boomed,
"If she leaves me, I'll say I'll leave her too!"

Now moods bloom brightly when they all were blue
and I've a line in jest where trouble loomed –
"If you leave me, I'll gladly leave you too."
(She thinks I'd do it but I never do.)

CRAQUELURE

Not being a soft habitué
of the halls of high art,
the man with the battered
sweat-stained hat – and, miles back,
his family given to spending
evenings on the verandah,
thanks to slim financial
readjustments at their bank –
surveys his land, squints
at fly-blown, bony sheep
as was ordained in better days
by past generations
when promise falsely rained,
cannot necessarily see,
though he sees all, that a network
of cracks on brown land
where the water's evaporated
stress an affinity
with the portraits of Leonardo
or Vermeer, the intricate
cracking on their paintings
beyond being halted
or, by the desperate, faked.

HEART ON A SUMMER AFTERNOON

Let me address you, heart, as a mate,
now beating hard after a quick
ascent of the hillside to where,
from this window, there's a view
to die for, if you'll excuse
an expression that smacks
of conflict.
             Ah, let's relax
by these moving curtains,
take in the air, consider
where we stand, how many
finite heartbeats we've expended
and, little drum, the number
yet to come. Hmmm.
May as well ask the date,
under this cloudless sky,
of the next outbreak of thunder.
You're a quiet one, though
I know electricity excites you.

Now I have my breath back,
many thanks, quite steady
along, I guess, with the swallows'
intake as they swoop, squeal,
and rise above the house, all
thoroughly in the present,
unlike the slow, reflective
humans on the nearby path.

Their perceptions, I'd tell the birds,
bypass the gravitational pull on glass
or, for that matter – in case
they'd think we're dilatory –
the rise of mountains and the seas,
tectonic shift across the planet,
especially since to swallows
a target summer fly moves
like a Zeppelin in their sight.

Heart, constant mate, I perceive
— now I rest on the grass outside —
there's no hurry or need
to cram in more Homo sapiens
things this summer and ape
the swallows' frenzy. The African
beat you keep in my chest
is great; we're sunned and fed —
as if, in this equatorial heat, vast
Europe might still be the risky
domain of strange primeval forest.

MR HABITAT ON TERROR ETCETERA

I go to the supermarket. Terror
of value-added crap and wasteful
packaging – a small theft
detected at the check-out
where the innocent might get arrested.
No stress. I glide my trolley
along fabulous canyons,
strata of brands,
in a kind of wild disconnect,
liberty here at its best, set,
over the speaker-system, to easy-
going tyrannical music.
Somewhere, somewhere
here in the West, I can see
– passing the refrigerator –
lock and key, swarthy citizens
held in some dark
deep-freeze. No release. Among
the beetroot and beans, I'm obsessed
with injustice, my one sullen
act to liberate a cabbage.
I hum. I push on. I could be
an innocent man who, on seeing
the arrival of police, starts to run.

THE HEATHROW TO MELBOURNE FLIGHT

for John Lucas

No better place to reflect when the yolk
moon's at the window, thanks to Qantas
and aerodynamics –
                      a mere day
to travel, book in hand, half way round the planet
and delay rising tax

on the atmosphere and dark forests. To be obedient.
Belted in. Dream a bit, think of how
where you've lived with the neighbours
is now in row 58 your exclusive domain.

To make elbow room prime space
above a desert where there's a track
and the promise of slow traffic. No better way

to save hours. Quite so, as you fly eastward,
your sun implies, rising for the price
of two appearances, three times.

No better place to exercise,
otherwise the celebrity horror, thrombosis,
might make a fuss, even
in first class and prove more expensive.

This, and the endless cuisine, while you're flying
in what seems the world's biggest intestine,
serve to emphasise this is where you now live

and how you wish to continue to do so –
asleep perhaps, or absorbed, during this novel
length flight, in classic fiction. At one sitting.

FREDDY AND THE CHRISTENING GIFT

What kind of life did the nuisance aunt
think the kid was in for, blessed and wetted
from the font, when she bought for him
an initialled napkin ring?
While she looked on the future was set,
fighting gear to the right and left of meat and veg,
napkin ever at the ready –
and then, post-skirmish, rolled
with spillage through the ring-hole.
He became the boy who could push
the napkin neatly through,
unsoiled, approved –
a victor who outgrew, like a stammer,
bad table manners, a credit
to the christening gift.
Folded, rolled, pushed it through
the silver ring, an endless exit.
Till, impatient, it's morning
papers he's rolling into plastic
to fling at addresses, rolling
cigarettes to thin perfection while
on a roll with a girl
still at school. It folded.
But not the supply in bars of slopped beer
he sopped up all through uni
till, salaried, his crisp initials on documentation
for the Saturn Debt Collection Agency
– a dirty business but we all must eat –
seemed prefigured by the gift,
he thought later, having quit.
He'd found the tarnished ring among
other outmoded things – polished
his appearance and folded
into his another life. A wife.
She was iron hot and he was pressed
to wipe for good the spittle
from her mouth, when there were guests.

Public servants, small guys churning
in the great machine of State he'd entered
– she called them serviettes –
ever now dispensable.
She craved for him adventure
to get, he reckoned, some less couth types
into the house, and besides
she'd had her bedtime fill of hearing
crude arguments for determinism
and against free will. They spilled
over into breakfast, like grain –
with the notion some piddling influence
can be multiplied by a crazy factor
and crease, fold and roll up a life
as if for its own furthering in a rain
– dear God! – of puns. So he escaped
to the whale-rich sea, a desert
where the law's a smoking gun,
a horror jungle; found a river
that stank from cowboy exploitation
of its banks – could soon relate
across a table stir-crazy dreams
or how to blow a mint in a bordello,
steal a masterpiece and give the finger
to CCTV. Viz, he became a reader.
In fact, a gathering. Relaxed,
bad-mannered as any character
that really mattered. Brash.
Fancied himself, in the bathroom mirror,
with a beard, on a life raft to his wife.
What a spin! Till he became polite again –
took the fallout like a paper napkin.

YOU ARE HERE

the sign says to him on its map, in red,

bright day, gateway to the park,
while Canada geese fly overhead. The words
imply he's fortunate, free to be
at large and see, through dark glasses,
others also at their ease. Or he takes
the statement for a stretch towards
a general meaning – that asserts
he, a walker, is alive on earth
when in his psyche that might seem
to be at the remotest border, more a rumour,
of where here is – then the simple
confidence of the sentence
might provide a double service.

There he marvels at the steady verb
that balances on either side companion words,
manages their nomadic weight. Or
sees the sentence as being omnipresent
and soon it finds him cold and wet
before a sign where he half-recalls starting
twenty years before. The words
only need an exclamation mark
to seem a greeting! No-one
begging for food or shooting: here
improves when elsewhere deems it good.
Now at a lookout, next
in a subway station. Others
are making translations: *Siete qui,*
Vous êtes ici, Usted está aqui.
Then in the mosquito-friendly heat,
he's reading: *Anda si gini,*
and he wants a swim, a martini.
Will he ever under his breath repeat
in Esperanto: *vi estas tie ĉi*
and, if so, where on earth

would he be? Not lost, surely, a pronoun
in its mini-utopia of the written word.
Go, the signs propose, from this spot
and so he does, now with his family,
now with a backpack, and soon
coming upon another attractive
You are here map, he's fleetingly affected
by a mild nostalgia but, search him, cannot
locate when for or remotely where.

DANDELIONS

The sun never sets on the empire of the dandelion.
Alfred Crosby

Sunbursts on a late
afternoon lawn, where gin might be served;
or they're back between cracks
like national borders in the concrete
and won't be extracted, the tap
roots fattening on a mixture
of blind persistence
and victory. Ever thus –
seeds airborne, arriving like parachutes
since the Cretaceous, light
of a hundred million
of the Earth's solar revolutions
inspiring them, filament
bright. High time,
– now children blow off seeds –
their advance was arrested,
the gardener thinks, annually
defeated, his new shed, the armoury,
his insult, to call them a weed.

AUGUST

Boot prints crisscross, oystercatchers
in the shallows keep their activities
distant, truants at any approach.

None, all day, will have managed
to get close — not even the horse
and its rider, hoofprints in the sand

made when the sunshine had warmth.
An aeroplane like an inspector,
above the pale ocean, also departs.

There are two people it can see,
late arrivals, shadows pointing east,
but won't notice, as a raptor might,

the eagerness on their faces, the flush.
Only the oystercatchers retain an interest,
self-interest in a rising tide, make one short

flight after another — from our perspective,
below the plane, comical and needlessly furtive.
The approaching dusk will suit them,

a winter dusk, early, our wild heat
independent of August sun.
Unexpected arrivals, late, the birds

surely reckon, and surely they'd
be correct, no-one now on the weather side
of the dunes likely to emerge today,

so blind and so radiant, breeze-blown
 — the breeze increasing — in a tangle
of scarves. We might be headed, right now,

arm in arm, down a platform
at a grand station, lovers pressing forward
through a crowd in the Age of Steam.

ROCK MUSIC

Turn off the radio, give it a break
from its anxieties, the up-to-the-minute
clashes and crashes, riots
and revolutions –
                let it ponder, up
there on the shelf, the way to alliterate
a rave about the power of a long pause
between three-minute pop songs.

Take off your wristwatch
and leave it as a gift. The card can say to whoever:
Here, have all the time that you want.

You want, having done this, to tune
into the frequencies of stone,
so many varieties can be reached
with a little ingenuity, here and now,

easy to find sandstone, harder
to reach schist and, if you can handle
the pressure, flint.

Soft rock, hard – marine
fossils, evergreens, can weather the tones
of blow-in aficionados. It will be

a very long session. A minute
representing millennia. Elsewhere
you, as audience, facing Triassic strata,

may get transported by sediments
bound together like pages that predate
the break-up, layers
of the supercontinent Pangaea. Read

about Geology in its infancy
and it's clear it couldn't have predicted
such widespread reception – the lovely stone
of cathedrals soon as much of a hit
as the bishop in his pulpit.

Next, to sex things up, let meteorites
be received – the one in the museum, prized
on its plinth as the Venus de Milo, marble
conceding to busy carbon, and getting
the attention an exotic rock
creates while it signals, mysteriously, all
it can about how life modestly began.

INTERROGATIVE PRESSURE

Then, one day, after decades
of risk and tearing up of tickets,
you snaffle a small prize
in a raffle –
        a teddy,
as it happens, rather too late

and think, on the spot, why me?
Followed by its interrogative
corollary – the one Dusty
Springfield posed when confirming to a journalist
she had cancer – me, why not?

If the prize
had been the latest Saab, would each question
somehow have been larger?

As conceivably on that day
you didn't catch the flight that didn't crash
but might have if you with your long-term tendency,
ditto you and you and you, to be the world's
great loser, had been on it –

making either rhetorical
query at 20,000 valuable feet above
the Pacific Ocean and fast
declining, imminent history.

But you are safely here now,
living in the slipstream
of a win, and feeling lighter
of heart and mind, the universe
– a dog-eared *Aristotle* on the table –
having contrived, in its unlimited
priming of probability to load,
for a couple of bucks, your dice.

That bear is more than a mere yellow teddy –
whichever fated kid you favour
with it is one day going to sit
an exit exam in metaphysics.

Years earlier, she'll wake up,
having named, loved, then
outgrown him, and faced
with a compulsory hearty breakfast
before her classes, one
or two of interest, she, the smartarse
will ask any dumb adult within
hearing, once and for all
 – after localised whydidyou interrogations –
for the sheer bloody-minded
hell of it, the subliminal
conundrum, and the looks
it must darkly bring to her folks'
lived-in faces, *Why –
why is there anything?*

CHANGE OF ADDRESS BOOK

Who's in, who's out?
In the old book there's about
a small town population, grown beyond
its limited accommodation –
pages no longer bound
to tell a meandering story
of the many restless
with crossed-out addresses.
Time to consign it to the bin
and pick future contacts.
Those, that is, still among
the living who've survived
the danger of being listed,
or have at some point
– queerly – disappeared
into other pages with some
equally alien company.
The inclusions are gamely
self-selecting – and checking
the entries it's absorbing
as free association
to recall visits to strange cities:
hunting, after dark,
for an apartment number,
or those addresses
where letters, sometimes
not all for others, had stamps
a resident, young philatelist
might briskly steam. One is now
an executive in New York City
and must recall the lonely trip
with the dreaming adults
along the river. Now it's quick
as pressing an ignition
to exclude the duplicitous
shit listed under *T*,
or to repress the prat whose surname

should have been exactly that.
And what of the address
 — *should you ever wish to visit* —
in old Mexico? Yes. And yes and yes
to all the welcome others who,
one expects, will never need
to flee a street, like Freud's
family when it quit Vienna.

PROBABILITY ETCETERA

What incalculably small chance
is there, in a mega-city
you visit, of meeting
on a bus someone who days
earlier you've emailed regrets
about failing to squeeze
him into your busyness – and besides
you've now lost his address –
with this limit-the-damage rider
"perhaps our paths will cross,"
the rising inflexion
heading like the number 55
up a High Street to where
such an improbability
finds its answer in a remarkable
widening of eyes.
                    This
occurrence on the day before
you woke early, refreshed,
the light sizing up the guest room
and, for that matter, you, Adam naked,
propelled by a unique
arrangement of genes,

thinking, with lax actuarial gravity
in the shower, about forebears,
plagues, wars, chance meetings,
the sperm and egg – somewhere –
that in all likelihood, way back,
escaped wedlock etcetera,
and sum you up.
                And therefore,
in past prospect, the clear improbability
of this morning being yours
 – or hers in the next room,
the neighbours', mates', callers', all
God's children – in particular to see it

with what is now retrospective
inevitability. Necessity calls
and you flee the figuring
to feel embodied again in clothes
and identity – start
into the wild light of this day
with a gait that might in a descendent
risk replication a century hence.

THE STORY OF A STORY

Who knows if the right occasion
will arise again to recall the morning
at the Victoria market, beginning
"Once when I ..." my heart-rate faster,
wide of a binding story of the nation,
for this, about how a bloke in front of a deli
dressed shabbily for winter in summer,
reached on tiptoe over the polished
glass counter into the bounty, salami
and cheeses, and grabbed a handful
of sausages – the white-coated
deli-owner's back to him as she piled
the meats she was slicing. Then
I'm virtually a student again, staring
 – compliments of the telling's renewable energy
lights shining freshly on cheeses – a vehicle
compelled to carry forward the story
to where the alkie in mid-grab
finds his handful is amazingly linked
to the dozens piled on the dish,
miles of them, no kidding, all suddenly
for the hauling before a small, rooted audience.
However, this is the story of the story
 – no stopping its opportunism, or for whom
it will be told – of the chain of sausages
coming up and over the counter,
until the complete haul for the dero
is the only way forward. So wait...
the shopkeeper's sad version
would simply relate how she
was confounded by a space,
empty white dish, next to the cheeses.
But by then the story was ready-made –
the bulging overcoat, the sausages
trailing the getaway through shoppers
were great – and apart from
the shopkeeper's face, no detail escaped.

KNIGHT

When I saw her, slender and taut,
as if for the first time
in the steamy bathroom,

turning away from the mirror,
so separate, hair still wet,
no sudden storm

could do it better, her body
pale at the end of winter
yet lithe as a dancer

set to clarify an emotion,
wide eyes entering the next
necessary preparation,

I took no ridiculous out-of-place steps
to protect her, was strengthened
by reckoning how soon

she'd meet whatever fiasco,
savvily dressed and, as any shield
can't be, readily animated.

THE SPIDER IN THE KITCHEN

I fed the spider beef.
Summer flies
in town were oddly few.
The spider took it in her stride,

tackled the bloody meat
with her black legs and due
surprise. She liked it.
Mince, match head-size, soon

burned in her abdomen. She thrived
and bred, though I never saw
her dark stranger call. The babies
were little monsters, big

and hungry. I obliged. Fillet steak.
No-one else now entered
the lovely kitchen – until,
one day, a wise guy

– distant relative in his teens –
who'd got wind of my arachnids,
looked down on me and from
his core, swore in a baritone

it was the hormones in the meat.
His bent head proved the ceiling now
too low. The spiders stretched
themselves across wide windows.

I looked heartlessly into their eyes.

THE FIRES
i.m. Margaret Scott

From the plane I see, leaving
after a brief visit, the smoke of bushfire,
summer's signature, figuring where to go.
There was a time the island seemed
close as I could get to home –
and you, Margaret, would say,
in your splendid town, then country house,
"Now tell me what you've been doing
and where you've been." Motherly,
it felt, smoke rising from cigarettes.
Two of your houses were reduced to ash –
the light of landscape, sea and sky
gushed through the wide
windows of your resurrected last.
Deprecating, droll, you might have said,
"nature can be a little rash,"
in your steady English voice,
gathering your already compact self
to outwit black catastrophe.
What a spirit! Fire appeared to nourish
the expression of it – manuscripts torched,
what you then needed was to exhaust
another pen and write the loved island
into haze-free focus, the mass-produced
thing facilitating a singular gift.
Another was your wit – brilliant
across a table or shared, on TV,
with the nation. You too were hot.
Amazingly, it also flared without
an appreciative listener to help inspire it
as when, late, on the long drive home
to the peninsula with its convict "stain"
and killings, you shouted repeatedly,
"Elephants! Elephants!" to the marsupial dark,
thereby keeping yourself awake.
You gave a beautiful, haunted,
serious island a sense of humour

and, unforgettably, as now I look towards
the roadless mountains, a moral compass
the public and the press could follow.
Soon it will be sea beneath
the plane, and I'll not have stayed
and said, as if it truly mattered,
what I've been doing and where I've been.

GIVEN

After the news, after hours
at a computer, after – or before –
the spring storm, after weeks

of inaction, the removal
of shoes and lacing up
of boots, his one

planned act is to dig –
raise and let settle a dark flock
of sods. The first, against the odds,

not-so-intractable earth
at his service. The next
 – after a breather – confirms

the readiness and range of it.
Gigantic, the fresh spadefuls
of planet; wrecked worms

like swimmers fighting
incredible turbulence.
It is civilisation that disturbs

them – and the action
of a man who, having
its backing, gets immersed

in moving sidelong, heave
after heave, then reverses a step,
triumphant over weeds.

There, sweating, he no longer
knows where he is, some place
in the realm of his body;

its oxygen, the intoxicant,
a spear, in flight, might once
have denied him. Now, later

– decades, centuries –
the frontier sensibly fenced,
he is dealing with an insurgency,

minus a shirt, baffling
the name on the gate
which might easily be *Wyewurk*.

Each step, each repetitive
action, exposes his place
in a succession, relay

of energy, the spade
a continual winner for seedlings
and ample technology.

Out there, weight of the earth
shifts elsewhere as if many
diggers have merged into one

or, at least, gather to urge
him on, and deliver, instead
of a chore, a perennial rhythm.

THE ROUND

> ...*restless forever, and quite indomitable.*
> Weldon Kees, 'Insectae Borinquenses'

Mid-week, he left. Whoever said,
"It won't be the same without him"
could only guess what bright version
of him sped into the morning,
paid the taxi driver, hefted
the case, refused to take the change.

He caught a plane and read the news.
Someone soon would ask, in passing,
what he does, meaning *Who are you?*
Then he might think but not say,
 "Well, I'll let you choose!" the truth
already claimed by the past tense.

He eyed the future from a foreign bus
which lacked at least one shock absorber
to counteract the pressing fact,
in a well-lit metropolis,
that a change of scene can jolt
a life out of what it's been.

Here he stayed – for a while. Years.
Took up a former calling. Left.
Became a chef, a good painter –
later a pianist in an
exclusive club; crept home, well spent
like an indomitable insect.

Women, stylish, came and went.
He lingered for coffee, often,
at the central station, relished
his anonymity as he watched
the departures, ever restless,
plagued by tremendous consequence.

There must be, he thought, an end
to this other than in a strange city
where his life again would be recast.
He packed – and soon was back to try
on for size what some found vast,
the one he'd quit. It didn't fit.

THE MOSQUITO SATISFACTION WRAP

Not the satisfaction of clawing
a nail from a plank or the overnight
doubling of money; not the completing
of a thousand-piece jigsaw of a Brueghel feast
or ever, in a quiz, of being the most clever;
not the satisfaction of being six
with a strap of liquorice
or bluffing a bully, more than each
of these, more than leaping
into an aquamarine sea, more than keeping
a secret, or weeping with relief,
though this is closer, as is
a superlative crap, better than,
at last, sneezing though not better
than a Belgian wheat beer straight from the tap
or, for a secret agent, a trap;
these are closer, the satisfaction levels
overlap, maybe echo
snails' slow pleasure of relieving
a garden of its seedlings
but not the Romans' mass
appetite for blood, which is closer,
as is, if available, goose
prosciutto with duck liver parfait
and brioche, masticated slowly,
with fine wine devoted to an aquiline,
or any other nose globally
closer to the mosquito's devotion, though
love-making, delayed, on sand
still warm, moonlight on the sighing water,
is more like it, hot, and rates
with a twitcher's orgasmic satisfaction
at sighting an orange-bellied parrot
which is in the vicinity, and a guide
 – though still at a silent distance –
to the moaning relief of a mosquito,
devoted to population explosion,

when, poised as a sprinter on skin,
her driven proboscis draws sweet blood,
a slow stoned-eyed gutful, till she wings
clear of itch, and trickily of vengeance,
her parting gift to the diminished victim.

ODE TO WATER

Even the elliptical drip
on the tap, I praise, since it's clear that bottled water
from far and near, in the shops
 – mountain landscapes on the labels – proves
that it's precious

in spite of the forecast downpour
now freshening local cheeks, and amphibians,
as the rivers increase.

Water, from your value-added captivity,
this far distant from cholera,
I'd release you,
for it is the changes
to puddles and streams that reveal
you are fleet but with no cheery
song like a bird's to summon pity.

The drip, distant
relative to lake, hits
the sink, impatient
to quit

as I am to taste
clear, cold, restless springwater
after a climb, in it my reflection
truer than in any snap-
frozen hall mirror.

Water, your each molecule
in that first lake I greeted
called Galilee, and first flood, beneath the eyes
of a dove, contains mystery,
bonds like no other,

is in my blood. No wonder
I've often dangled my legs over the edge
of a jetty and stared
long into your depths.

Pindar said, thinking of drink,
water is best, and no doubt
that's also the opinion of clouds.
I wouldn't think
of spoiling a rare measure of it
with malt whisky.

Or let my patience
evaporate in the vicinity
of a common drip.

Since, water, you make up
the bulk of me; as surely
as a diviner's willow switch sensing the deep
you draw me to bathe in the sea,
or the sick to the waters
of Lourdes, all of us going
via a primordial link
to ocean beginnings.

 In the drip I now praise
 – whose molecules may have visited all rivers,
rinsed off the shit poured out from cities,
and are here freshly
united – there are bonds
to continuities no spanner
will interrupt when the tap's fixed,
and therefore soon a desire,
as if daft, to walk through a downpour
without an umbrella.

from The Bicycle Thief & Other Poems (2013)

POSTCARD TO HAMBURG

The postcard, never sent, arrived.
Theresa, who wrote it in German
during or after a visit to Canterbury
– sunlit cathedral in the photo –
intended to send it but, in London,
the card had vanished.
                        Nevertheless,
Frank in Hamburg read its message – to,
when she heard of it, Theresa's wild surprise.
The card now seemed as likely to be
in one place as, at the same time, in another,
revealing in a world where classical physics fits
something of what strangely happens
when attention is on the subatomic.

I couldn't be grasped and pictured –
and for as long as they might speculate,
the two won't get a grip on the miracle
that happened to connect them. I hope
they're now emotionally closer.
                            The pavement
was dry when I spotted the cathedral,
expecting, reverse side, some old message;
found a fresh one, active stamp
– me, a mystery agent (call me Fate)
reading but understanding little, quick
to find a postbox and, through the slot, drop
the card from my newly invisible hand.

STONE INCLINATIONS

Even mudstone has its clarities –
silt's soft landing, the ocean floor
compacted, marine life there

for future reading; the Triassic fishes
so freshly expressed, the days
of their expiration seem, even in a museum,

strangely transparent. Cracked open,
mudstone gives an answer, not hard,
to a palaeontological question. Ask,

next to uplifted sedimentary strata,
the location of the ocean beneath which
its aeons of memory accumulated

and the answer, on a calm afternoon,
might test the questioner's balance – duly awed
before what truly has risen. How fleeting

and small our comprehension seems –
a stone thrown into the ocean is as deeply
responsive to forces. Granite foreshore,

from where it may have been launched,
is an impenetrable door, thick,
into the Earth's molten core, miners'

explosives might pester like callers.
Then an invitation to a mansion
with polished stone floors may be about

as cool as granite gets – so refined,
it facilitates social, if not geologic,
understanding. Elsewhere, deep underground,

marble is forming. Is it harder to get a grip
on things metamorphic? – to dance to the tunes
of gneiss and schist? We know how flint

Stone Age implements came about but not,
for sure, how flint originates in a
limestone region – then in enduring form

for mediaeval walls. It's a pretty
mystery. One way or the next, all things morph.
Homing in – at an analogical stretch –

on a genome of stone, creates for us a pause
in the geologic process, to absorb perhaps
how time passes for a boulder.

Or the metamorphosing quartzites. Right
now the lump bought at a market stall
is refracting light and looking lively.

Though it's diamonds that fire
a frenzy of inclinations; condensed
in the lot are the majority of geological epochs

not necessarily lost on the guy who, dazzled
by a woman's eyes, says with a grin, "Hey,
that's a nice rock on your digit." No other gem

so radically slows the speed of light.
Or chimes with a wish that knowledge
of this flawed and opaque business

of existence might suddenly become hard,
cold and immaculately clear – for anyone
obsessed by possibilities beyond his reach.

BEATING THE CHINESE

I played table-tennis against the Chinese
and sweated most. What make-up
makes them so cool? Nevertheless
I had them on the run and, let's get
it over with, mostly won.

They seemed impressed,
I was surprised, rapt to outclass them
on their home patch. I kept mum.
In any case, perhaps the watchers
thought they were hallucinating
a rehearsal for a laughter industry. The ball
was our way of communicating –
while showing how to manage energy –
though I couldn't then easily get why
my opponents often missed it
as the polite Chinese
clapped at my expertise using a well-worn bat.

I whacked the ball so it angled badly
off the perimeter of the table – dashed
this way and that, catching,
at each serve, my breath; something
the opposing players, half my age,
didn't need to match. I paused,
bounced the ball, created the kind
of tension that mounted as hot Beijing
awaited the announcement that would say if it
would boast its own Olympics.

No points for guessing who'd roast
all opponents at table-tennis.

                                       In retrospect,
this makes my surprising form now worth recording.
Some games I bashed
the ball so hard, it cracked.

Others, I cut and curved it, almost,
as the ball spun above the table, made it stall –
slyly varied my attack, ever
improving the spectacle by crashing
into one or another wall.

It was a small venue, nicely
containing the cries for more balls
served with the hoped-for effect, on the opposition
of knocking back local rice wine minus food.
I wouldn't be surprised if a wrecking ball
a little later flattened the place, a release –
kept moving through the neighbourhood,
demolishing any keen opposition,
in a display of sudden energy.

SPEED & OTHER LIBERTIES

Off season, 2005, in Iceland, the highway
has no business crossing a treeless, ashen flatland.
Not required, except for the hire car
I happen to be driving, testing the limits
of isolation. The appearance of another
would surprise. One does, of course, a dot
approaching. Nearer, uh-oh, it's the police.
I'm writing, at the time, *Speed & Other Liberties*.
The Land Rover goes by, U-turns, is soon behind.
I reason the officer needs me for relief.
Window down – it's freezing – it's as if I've seen
his uniformed chest in other, far away locations.
He wants to be reacquainted.
I'd like to shout – now I'm ticked off – aren't there
any crims round here, hiding out? But need
my liberty to finish the new book quickly.

DESERTER IN THE COUNSELLING ROOM

Under the cover of darkness, plus
streetlights, Walker left with a shoulder bag,
plastic cards and cash.
                                  He felt bad
slipping out of the uniform
– the way he saw it – of marriage,
kids, a job and the safe
street that could not contain him.

At a guess, I could see it
in his genes, restlessness, a line
of bolters dating back to a medieval village
long since flattened; an archaeological
prospect under grazing land –

a forebear itching to settle
on whether to fight for King
or Cromwell, and then escaping
into the privations of a dense forest.

Anyway, some imperative that's been at work
way off anything I could put my finger on.

Walker, at war with himself and mystified,
maybe had the Nuremburg Principle
in mind and thought
of the awful consequences,
wreckage, heartache
and haranguing, should he stay.

The hard thing is, it's now months since
he's moved his debit card and – I'm guessing –
his mobile phone is long since drowned
in the Pacific Ocean.

                        When I think of him
I myself begin to vanish
 – if you're still with me, Angela –
cling to the chair where I'm there to listen.

One thing is certain
now the astounded family
are better off without him
 – not true, of course, but I'd like your view –
he's a man who can approve and deliver
his own flogging, and on his face
wear the pain like a tattoo.

MARVEL

Unexpectedly, one morning, I'm being driven fast
to Great Village, Nova Scotia, where as a kid
Elizabeth Bishop lived – went into the clapboard house,
went up to the little room where she slept, or tried to,
the sleep of a nascent poet. While, downstairs,
her grandparents snoozed by the Little Marvel Stove.
Now forever gone! I looked down at the narrow bed,
up at the skylight right above it, home
of the travelling Milky Way, while nearby roamed
 – or soon would – the moose she'd see from a bus
and, with a transcontinental pen, take
a modest twenty years to make, suddenly, marvellous.

THE OTHER LIFE
for Christopher Reid

It continued snowing.
The furniture hadn't drifted away in a removal van.
We kept Sam. We didn't catch a taxi
to Heathrow. The hi-fi kept going.
We didn't fly twelve thousand miles.
We stayed at home.
My father continued working in the City.
My mother lived.
She called into the morning, staccato,
"SamSam, SamSam, Sam" and he grew fat
on his diet of Kit-e-Kat.
I remained the "I" I'd got to know.
Next winter the snow
was even deeper. 1963. Soon, The Beatles.
I changed schools and tried to manage the terror of exams.
I expanded my collection
of geological specimens from the solid British Isles,
had good manners at the dinner table, a proper accent.
Elsewhere, out on my bike, I deferred
to words like "berk" and "blimey".
My mother continued to be unstable.
Wept. My father read the *New Statesman*.
They said, maybe it would've been better to get away.
We managed Paris. I smoked fags.
"Love is all you need", I sang, and fell in love.
I'd stopped praying. Prayed.
Existentialism was the rage.
Further on than this, as if in a pea-souper,
the other life gets small and blurry.
Except in it, reminded, I think of flying return
to summer in Australia
– though our winters now are milder, clearer –
to get a hint of what might have been,
unfreeze a kind of parallel existence.
I let it drop, overnight, like rainwater.

LOOSE AT THE ZOO

The gates are open. The crowds have suddenly moved away.
The zoo is now a past attraction. Walk into the ark

at your leisure, with undiminished fascination,
and notice the signs to the featured creatures:

giraffes, snow leopards, chimpanzees, gorillas.
Prefer the shady side of the approaches.

There remain birds in the callistemons and eucalypts.
Be very wary. On a metal gate, there's a sign:

No Public Access. It too is open. You push it further,
undisturbed. Rubbish that won't be collected –

a chimp is rifling through it, hungry; a relief
to see, released, he's now your equal. Leave him to it.

It seems the ancient Aldabra tortoises will, like boulders,
never leave; conceivably they're still in Africa.

Then, suddenly, on a fence, there's a macaw,
red-bellied, no, two, the other blue and gold

on a branch above. They both eye you as they would
a tourist blundering through Brazilian jungle, him

in camouflage, them in colours that suggest
an outrageous sense of humour. No danger, yet –

it's the big cats that make caution a defence
that's meagre, especially as your mind wanders

back to when you were small, hands on a rail,
and watched caged energy, pacing, a giveaway

flick of a tail, soliciting awe. By now, in the south
of the zoological gardens, you see Sydney harbour

below, empty of activity, and there in a haze,
the shoreline city. Smoke. Ah, a group

in a rowing boat making away
from the catastrophe, another clutch of skyscrapers

where the future was made. A tiger
is at your throat. Thirst. Delirious

or in a dream you're where something must be done
to quench it but what will, right now, is not available

to logic. Circling, overhead, there's an Indian condor.
Whoever had the keys and with foresight released

the creatures has, presumably, fled to protect
whatever possessions she has left. The aviary that houses

the hooded robin, the variegated fairy wren
– native species of the region – is empty.

Perhaps a barking owl swooped in, though it prefers
to pounce on birds its own size or, admirably, bigger.

Somehow, now, it would make sense
to round up the creatures and put them back,

confound the situation and watch yachts
released, fully spinnakered, into the harbour,

see the city as it was – see through
child eyes again the agile chimps but, oh,

the thirst, and then the distraction as you yelp
at an approaching brown-eyed lioness about to leap.

IN THE VILLA GORILLA

Midday, he's eaten his greens
and fruit, shoots, to get himself focussed,
a game of pool, and wins. He's not
a lonely ape. For reading,
this intellectual swinger needs his glasses.

He's working on a thesis about
why non-human creatures feature strongly
in kids' literature, and in adult,
weakly. At his desk
he sure looks powerful;

knuckles down around the house,
is a bit of a kid himself. Getting about
is how he gets his inspiration,
not being a believer in hanging around
and waiting.
              What exercises him
is the notion that human adults
grow away from a relationship
with great things around them – superior brains,
up near their ceilings, dismiss
an interest in, say, ants or snakes. Serious

thesis which shows how they look down on kids,
nostalgic, and humour them
with a lot of colourful, talking animals.

This is what keeps him busy, up
till what for him is late, while tired humans
are busy reading their kids to sleep.

It makes him snort to think about it.
He takes a break. He sings
his favourite song, which begins,
"Big gorilla in the L.A. Zoo
snatched the glasses right off my face"

by Warren Zevon, thinks
he inspired it. Yep. Look what he's wearing.

Now, he's occupied by exceptions –
spread before him, books by Bishop,
Hughes and Lawrence; among fifty poems
he knows by heart, the long one about the moose.
There are birds galore, bats, mosquitoes,
but what grates on him is the lack
of apes, especially when
his sympathetic take on the preoccupations
of the poets, judged on how they
lived, shows each was really a grown-up kid.

He loves them, nevertheless, relates.
Soon he's going to create a chapter
about how animals were not lost
on God and, especially, not on Noah
and his family – a great Bible story,
including apes, made when
civilisation was still in shorts,
and now foreseeably may expire,
which he thinks is telling.
                        But for today,
after drinks and dinner, some light
musical relief, he's read enough
about the human species to get him some sleep.

JACK AND YVES AND THEIR MANY TRANSPORTS

Train! Jack calls out once
and once again. He lives
near a railway station.

He stops. His index finger
is a little wand. Transport
attracts his first vocabulary.

Elsewhere, he's soon
thrilled to exclaim *car!*
bus! bike! as they whizz by

and since both parents
have their eyes on him,
he surprises them, or me,

with a high-pitched *plane!*
raised eyebrows an immediate
family feature. Jack's delight

in speed is cheerful news
for the petroleum industry.
For his cousin, Yves

– he has one tooth, not yet a word –
I wish a preoccupation
with modest yachts

he'll spot at sea
near where he lives, the wind
inexhaustibly clean, the oceans

rising. One yacht, decades off,
on which Jack and Yves may be seen
tacking through holiday waves.

MARINE DESIRE

There on my window sill, a fossil –
the solid echo of a bivalve, dry
and distant from the ocean.

It took the whole evolving
ecosystem to give it life –
the moon and tides, the tiny organisms
needing light, marine desire, the mix
of molecules to give it muscle
to shut its shell and ever-so-cleverly
open it again, when necessary.

Darling, our love approached
extinction in tight
confines with their clocks
and curtains, the can't-be-helped
restrictions; tried to adapt
to that interior even when
exhausted of mutual oxygen.

THE BICYCLE THIEF

The absence, next to the wall,
was exactly the size
of my bike. So let me fill you in.
It's a ten-speed Wanderer, blue,
no guards, some rust
on the handlebars, fairly useless
brakes, in a crisis. Passed
on to me, free, to see
if I'd again take to riding – the likely
final owner. Wrong. It was gone.
The sun shone on the spot
where I saw it not
in actuality but as the shape
of my dismay. We'd got on – fast.
I hovered there awhile,
as if the last few minutes
could be rerun without
the appearance of a thief.
It is me not him, the monkey,
who is missing from the scene;
now he's beat it on a good thing
with a quick getaway
built in. I hardly appear
to still be there, threatening
as vapour to him, a light
fingered guy, barely approaching
the fringes where great headline
crime gets real traction.
You know the type. He needs a bike,
old or otherwise. He's got
something on his mind. Spots
my good-for-the-planet
transport, sans lock – who'd bother? –
and after a swift swivelling
of his head to check for the idiot
who's left it – the only
time I move him – is off,

left down Clarke Street, then
right down Rae, I'd guess, cruising
along to the High Street shops.
It's still super hot at 4 p.m.
He needs a cold drink.
I know the feeling. He flips
the top, slyly sips, but can't
get away from behind
the crisps display without paying.
He slams the coins down on the counter,
raises the can and gulps the lot.
The transaction has almost
cleaned him out. Meantime,
the bike, propped against a council sign,
is obedient as a dog. You'd recognise it
from my opening description,
just as sure as he knows
he won't be followed. Who'd bother?
A police helicopter, if there were one,
would now see me hoofing it home,
so far away from stealing bits
of his lingo, he'd have a further
reason to feel shielded. Now he's off
again, he's owed some dough
for homework, actioned
by his aunt, while his uncle
was in the slammer. The house
is pages of the street
directory away – grand
compared to the tip his mum lives in –
which he can navigate as if
at birth he was equipped
with Google Earth. But first,
more urgently, there's a bird,
a chick, a bit of skirt
– or some term on a recycling list –
that he must see, where she works
in a nearby pharmacy. He knows
when it closes. Soon. With the big hand
of the town hall clock moving

at a speed unknown when he idled
through exams, he zooms
downhill on old reliable
whose tyres, in fair condition,
I found en route required some air.
At home, the pump. So,
his bum is alert to every
crevice in the road. But on
he goes, freewheeling
through the heat – wonderful feeling –
that leans on the stalled
and guzzling motors, till he sees,
unique as Eden, the pharmacy.
You'll now recall my estimation
of the brakes. For me, who gripped,
sat tight, lowered my head
in a racing pose – I rekindle
this as I walk home – while
giving the bike its freedom
on downhill tracks, no bother.
The kid's in traffic. The pharmacy's
at an intersection. The lights are amber,
no, red. He squeezes
the brake levers and continues
speeding. Thinks quick. Rears up
the bike, half pirouettes it
to the right, and rides
old reliable like a monocycle
among amazed pedestrians
to the kerb – a feat he briefly hoped
would impress the bird.
The first glimpse he gets,
through the window, is of her long hair,
so dark, it emphasises the white
of her uniform. Then she turns wonderfully
towards the street. He rests the bike.
Resumes breathing; removes the cap
he's been wearing backwards.
Bins it. Thinks: everything
in there looks slow. Enters.

She's not actually yet
his sheila, they're not yet
on first name terms, in fact
haven't really met, so although
much idiom has greased
his streets-long desire to see her,
he's lost for words where Revlon
and Estée Lauder make the place
feel foreign. He wants to be gone.
No, he doesn't. This is the first
time he's had the courage to go in.
She hovers beautifully in the realms
of his fascination, arranging
make-up stuff, when the plan
of action that began about
the time he saw my bike, strikes.
He'll buy something. What follows
is a fumbling that produces
an invaluable, last dollar
and a search for what it will
honestly convert into his own.
Nothing at first, or soon, until
he spies, on special, a nail file
which, in his hand, closely examined,
guides him to the counter.
The girl smiles, and so do all the models
in the framed cosmetics posters.
He'll forever keep the five cents
she gives back, says thanks twice
and, before he can meet her eyes,
is gone, relieved and satisfied.
No blunder. The nail file's stashed,
a present for his mother.
He retrieves his cap from among
overflowing ice-cream wrappers,
guns the bike in the direction
of his uncle. When it was made,
decades back, it was surely aimed
at this summer. There, for all
the sluggish rush-hour traffic to see,

it picks up speed, emissions-free,
the kid now aware
the tyres need air. I confess,
now I wish the pump had gone with it.
Your bike might be the one
he nicked the necessary from.
He gives it exercise, then his bike
which, with renewed traction, glides
during the ensuing hour past
three inviting features
he dangerously fixes
his eyes upon, amid the moody
homebound traffic: McDonald's.
The lad, you'll understand, is hungry.
He urgently pushes the bitumen
from underneath him, jerks
old reliable out into the loosening
stream to nick some speed
and, as a bonus, flirt
with death, an experience
so far, in all his years, in which
he's come off best — besides,
he's still thinking of paradise.
At this point, a caution might
be winged in his direction: his dad,
in a beat-up Valiant,
was not so lucky. Right now,
the kid's promethean, and the breeze
is with him all the way
to his rellies' street. The house,
postwar Melbourne brick veneer.
He dumps old reliable, free
for all to pinch, in the drive.
Who'd bother? If I'd tailed him
as he made it fit to be
his own ... A gum tree
guards the block. He knocks.
His uncle, sweating in his singlet,
admits him. There's the kitchen.
His aunt is busy — sees

her sister's kid. They both quiz him.
When he's able he tries politely
to turn the tables and bring
this family gathering around
to one thing. This will require
an unexpected depth of patience.
They're pleased to see him. He sinks
inwardly and grips a seat. Listens
to his uncle's plans post-release
from the can, remembering,
now he's the age
when the man before him
first got caught, never
to steal a fire engine. But what's
odder now is his uncle's rave
about going straight
and, while he was in the slammer,
his aunt cosying up to God
while holding down some kind of job.
No wonder his cousins
have done a runner, one
to Launching Place, another
to the Gulf of Carpentaria.
How, out of these weirdos,
is he going to get the money?
At last, some tucker. Absolute
concentration. Now he's being
asked how he got there
and what's the honour. Jesus!
His aunt's forgotten those hours down
on his knees among the weeds.
As he's seen in many a
gangster movie, he rubs together
his thumb and forefinger. His uncle
gets it. Translates. The missus
casts about for the wallet. Soon,
they're outside, standing around
old reliable. It's dusk. The shrill cicadas
are feverish. The lad explains
he got the bike off some random,

an expression lost, at first,
on his uncle after his years
removed from youth. That I feature
here doesn't mean he gets
the whole truth. Proprietorially,
uncle checks the brakes, exclaims,
"They're cactus, mate!" – a blindly
touché moment. The lad's face
is blank, masking a seismic
flash-back that proves where all can see,
they're stuffed. It then deflects
his aunt's kiss, since she's forgotten
who now he is – which leaves
him only to escape
his uncle but not, I fear,
his idiom when suddenly,
more himself, the guy
who at night can heist an ATM,
never, in his aunt's words,
having left the marriage bed, grunts,
"Stay on the outside, kid, inside
they're all a bunch of cunts."
Back on the drag, he gradually
stops, under a street light,
and counts the money. Some
for him and some, of course,
for his mother. The loot looks to be
in mint condition. He riffles it.
Wicked! There's one last major thing
now on his mind. He rears
the bike, out of the light, quickly
settles in to a marathon rhythm.
The night's his own: a few
cars on the road with lonely
drivers while he's in the singing
company of anticipation, closer
in remarkable time, to home.
Now, you and I are law-abiders
and would think little of it if, suddenly,
we're in the proximity of cops.

In fact, their car is right
beside him. He doesn't stop
at first, bothered again
by the brakes problem, though
eventually the bike obliges,
as the cops have wanted.
Oh fuck, he thinks, before the quiz.
I forgot to mention that the bike
lacks lights but these cops
are not so slack, and then they're
asking him where's his bloody helmet –
a matter, now I think of it, where
whatever unlikely things
the kid and I have in common,
here they perfectly unite.
He's on show, torchlight
on his face, exhibiting the frozen
features of the well-known –
watching a goon say, very clearly,
"You're a bad lot, you Muldoons, corrosive."
This sounds to him impressive,
especially since his dad, a big man,
liked to say, since 1788 the state
has shaped up to the likes of us,
like a bully. He's history
but the kid still hears him, and now
out of the spotlight, the cops
telling him to be off, to watch it,
to not get nabbed at night again, to finally
and etcetera hop it home to bed,
son, the brakes on their concern
at last working. OK. But first
to where he was going, more slowly
on the pavement, as at length directed,
though he reserves the right,
at intersection traffic lights
to ride against the "don't walk" signs.
Till rising off the seat, he shoves
his weight onto the peddles and, gliding,
times it so he stops exactly where

actuality and his mind again combine –
the bike shop, and there, for him,
the super model he longs for, shining.
He feels the wad of notes
in his pocket. Checks the price.
Reflects. Rechecks. Looks recklessly
down on old reliable between his legs
and thinks, honestly, why bother?
He's right. She's most impressive.
So is getting in various measures,
quickly, fame, the girl,
and the money – with my best wishes.

from Baffling Gravity (2019)

THE TILERS

Three of them, nailing down
   a geometry of slate. I'd be sorry
if they move on soon
   to some other leaky London roof.
I hear them, five storeys high, opposite,
   tap, tap, tap, over and over
like someone trapped under rubble, news,
   a catastrophe, the future of cities,
they don't count on beneath
   a Constable sky. They banter.
One sings "Blue Suede Shoes".
   I admire their footwork.
They don't look up as I do,
   from the window,
with a cultivated eye. Sensibly
   they look down – Euclid's their guy –
placing exactly each slate.
   Pitched roofs are a forecast of rain.
I look up, as if for the tilers, at the sky. Hmm.
   Maybe I'll have quit town, zipped
my bag, flown south before
   they've finished their expert resistance.
I'd be glad, though, to stay
   till they go, having viewed their roof
with as little gravity as I do
   a pavement – as I whistle
some old hit perhaps – exhibit
   a walker's brisk equilibrium, go
nowhere that stirs up vertigo.
   The tilers resist its attacks, exist like cats.
They show, startlingly, to those
   with a level nose for doom,
hey, that thing is never going to happen.

METEORITE

Maybe it was the streak
   of light in the night sky
some kid in a hinterland
   called a falling star opportunity
for a wish   maybe it doubled
   as a portent in the direction
of a priest maybe it dropped by
   at 10 p.m. local time
exactly   without doubt
   suddenly a hot rock   aeons
of momentum making certain
   it would be a special museum
attraction very welcome not often
   thereabouts to have the honour
the paying of respects by outer solar matter
   no knowing firmly where it's
been hanging out in exile
   since the scandal gangs of macho
cosmologists call the Big Bang some trip
   the bulk of the narrative
missing dark energy now
   ever in the background
a barren planet or two perhaps
   a cautionary feature   no guessing
how complex before the ore-laden rock's
   what-the hell-is-this-entry
into the rare atmosphere spectacular
   with lots to offer a full stop

AT THE HOTEL SPLENDIDE

There's a broad view of the sea
and key fobs are made of mahogany
at the Hotel Splendide.

Remember? Maybe not.
It may not be possible.
The five-bladed fan, mechanical insect,

in the dining room had possibly stopped –
out of consideration
for the weather, cool from hot –

and all the better to fix it
in mind. Time there never
is pressing. The staff are forgetful.

In the Hotel Splendide
the staff are discreet. For each passing guest
a private balcony's empty.

The four floors, the corridors,
the grand atrium with its Steinway piano
and calming palms are often mute

as a hospice at dusk
for the rich in *dishabillé* or whoever's
attendant blood roars on.

There are cocktails at the cost
of leaning high on a balustrade
between midday and nine.

None soon will remember.
Witness the mirrors –
the mirror ornately framed in the hall,

the long mirror in the lift,
the mirrors, two in each room –
the wardrobe, the dresser –

another, man-size, propped
for an epoch against a wall; mirrors
oval, oblong, and mantle ...

You can see, stepping past yet another,
the Hotel Splendide
is dedicated only to recalling itself.

There's a bold letter 'S'
in the antique tiles at the entrance,
on each fresh serviette,

and those who stay duly remind
themselves in the mirrors
– repeatedly – of actual guests.

QUARRY

Where the quarry you've come across
   was once, its nitrate explosions,
bulk rock thumping the ground,

wonderful shudders long over –
   and the gut masculine satisfactions,
the foundations for Federation houses

well settled, backgrounds perhaps
   for the remotest family photos,
faded, lost or boxed-up anonymous –

eucalypts have long taken root
   in the jagged artificial cliffs,
their damp fissures and cracks.

We might say they "cling" to the cliffs,
   thinking of ourselves, looking up,
as being precarious

beneath the afternoon sunlight
   the trees distribute. These
or any species you see

are mostly invisible, namely
   how they were before now,
how they'll become awesome

to others, possibly in moonlight.
   Wherever you find yourself there's
only time, a little or a lot, to glimpse it.

GRAVITATIONAL PULL

Gravity always proves itself:
the climber falls, the pen drops;

an angry lover slams a door,
a glass topples off a ledge and shatters –

a constant, the gravitational attraction.
Gravitons, though unobserved, make sense

should they be there, blind
to Einstein's theory, defiant.

A wall collapses, a meteor
brightens the night sky. Balls of unequal mass

it's reported Galileo dropped
from the Tower of Pisa, a high

Renaissance demonstration, peaked
in a dead-heat. Equally,

when gravity makes sediment impressive,
the bedrock might well be reckoned

to express weight in falling, spent.
Newton explored the force, mostly indoors.

Only a featherweight
without room to exist in a big vacuum

could possibly make light of it.

TO CHARLEVILLE
for Leah and Tom

The overnight train journey to Charleville
not taken remains a sadly
forsaken opportunity. What difference
it would have made, what discoveries
might have occurred along the way,
I cannot know. For I refused to fork out
the excessive fare – a week's wages
for many a labourer – to reserve a designated seat
and sit up all night, rigid, as if attending
a remarkable lecture. At the Toowoomba
station I did not make an enquiry about the price
of a sleeping compartment. The train,
that night, would formally depart without me
and, I was told, most all of the seats
I could choose from would be empty.
This, I said politely to the man
in uniform, I can understand.
                                        The journey
not taken could have been to an outpost in Ethiopia
or one on a Russian steppe, or to some
other destination I'd lately researched,
a consequence of having personal business
in the region – some unvisited place
the locals don't consider to be remote,
an isolated cluster of lights
maybe seen from a plane at night –
but, on that recent day, it was to Charleville, Queensland
I didn't set forth with a flask of soup and a desire
to feel unleashed from care, acquire
whatever wisdom might come about
from travelling to a town where once,
in the main street, a man, deriding gravity,
fired cannons at recalcitrant clouds
in the hope of breaking a lengthy drought.

The expensive overnight train journey to Charleville
remains with me in past prospect – the vast
canopy of stars from the windows, the rhythm
on the rails of wheels, the meditative
journey with a fine excuse, like some
fabled island, to make it. Or, actually,
two supermarkets, three butchers
and two bakeries, the official website states
as attractions – and better still
"No one should go hungry in Charleville"
which skinny millions, jammed into carriage
after carriage, would applaud if they could ordinarily
make the trip. I was better off without a ticket.

EXPECTING THE SÃO JACINTO FERRY

The ferry, red contra white, was long delayed,
no reason offered. The sea was calm. Reflections
from the quay and boats periodically ran deep. Sunshine
was intermittent. Then, ropes released, the ferry left.
A half hour direct to São Jacinto, away
from the idle cranes and freighters; herring gulls whining.
This happened last April, time for the ferry to moor, its steel gates
parting for the residents and their small cars. Stray visitors.
The broad resurfaced esplanade – in sports track ochre –
was soon again deserted except for men, ex-sailors maybe,
sitting around an outside café table. Shadows
of the postcard palm trees were fan-shaped till cloud
erased them. Doors on the little balconies of the portside houses
stayed shut, the sea a clear disappointment. A visitor
would not seek to ask why the Esplanada Bar was closed
but wonder at the need, like a final insult, for the sign that says
ATTENÇÃO Proibido Pescar to tempt old
fishermen to be disobedient. The ferry left
to eventually reappear, always now too late to connect
with industry. On the Rue Dos Estaleiros the deco ship
equipment factory stands a wreck, windows all teeth, smashed,
gravity of the financial crash littering the dark interior. Other
monuments to past employment approach collapse,
roof tiles gone, walls cracked. No-one, or no-one visible,
except a stranded visitor, was fascinated or alarmed – since
what's happened to the folk around São Jacinto cannot attract
satisfactory understanding – by the men dressed in black, from
   boots
to balaclavas, who raided the ruins,
spilled out, weapons tilted (more strange emergency aid
from the European Union?) an actual Portuguese
commando attack – on whom? – or gun theatrics in anyman's-
   land
the enemy not then in April a brand of sunny economics,
the exercise complete in time for the troops' conveyance,
on the afternoon ferry, late, as expected
by the gloomy and gutted in that or any other month to come.

THE NIGHT JOURNEYS

Nightlights strobe through the window's
   condensation, signals from anywhere, a stratosphere,
      at 3 or 4 a.m. – sometime to find oneself suddenly

awake, making haste across a country
   that will forever contain others' breadth
      of residential moonshadow. Or an owl's. The train's

motion is all; sleep the only known border
   when travelling through such space. Then slowing to a halt,
      somewhere as gripping as grease, wheels seizing the rails,

as if a reason to continue on into the long night
   is duly being mustered, a wearisome matter.
      Sleep, then. The resumed rhythm of the train under stars

is a drug big pharma can't ever market.
   Horizontal, on a bunk, the idea of levitation
      gets close to how abandoned by gravity

the body, an addict, feels – where? – between
   a distant foreign point of departure and a vaguely
      understood destination. The train ticket admits

one traveller to erase hard distance itself,
   then memory of it. If transmigration is release, a vast belief,
      this surely must be like it, once, then repeatedly.

TAMARILLOS

Vertigo is nowhere
where they are, and time,
too, seems suspended.
Ovoid, working on ripeness
dozens make no demands
on the branches, light,
they might be, as blown eggs,
easily out of reach among
the sunlit leaves. Tamarillos,
tree tomatoes, *tomates de árbol*
or whatever name holds them aloft
in a nation's esteem, these
exotics, close to the window,
are merely mute absorbers
of birdcalls and banter,
no-one's gift to cuisine;
a slow over-the-summer
accumulation, providing
silence with a shape
like a form of percussion
never to be struck.
In their plenty they are polished
and smooth experts
at deferment, unusually
snobbish. Elsewhere, in rows,
they're a crop. The
compelling force, it's
beneath them to address,
they hourly thwart; another lofty
thing that makes the fruit look
so perpetually good –
who'd wish to pick any? –
until the first one drops.

SOURCE

1

Shifting, the source of the river begins
in run-off and seepage, far from here,
a forested upland; the named and un-named
tributaries to its south-east concede,
at each confluence, to the Yarra, its downflow,
at this place, in late summer, steadily slow.

Call the river's course "progress",
which it offered when, on the north bank,
a colonial mill pounded; the first Homo sapiens,
around the valley, by then haunting a silence.

All the global water that's flowed since Dight
built his mill goes smoothly over his weir.

It was never intended to be, but is, soothing to hear.

2

The perpetual sound of water falling
intensely, yet what the sandstone cliffs
make of this place has memorable depth, its source
the sediments trapped four-hundred-and-twenty
million years back, give or take some, under
a Silurian sea.   The strata look fresh, neatly
layered, undulate like long waves.
The motion of the uplift caught, it seems,
by the afternoon light, next to the river,

well above the lost ocean it's come clear of;
journeying creamy rock – lightweight enough,
given a little tectonic force to do
the hauling – an epoch shown, in a squeeze.

3

As it happens – causality nascent – a saxophonist
stood, when eventually spotted, at a high confluence
of geologic and historic time, on the cliffs
overlooking the river.
                                    His instrument glinted, tiny.
Shirtless, he shone. The low notes flowed, as if
a far off source informed them, then rose some distance –
the sound of the water falling close to those few
who heard him, improvising, like the course of a river.
He sought no audience, no more than does a Silurian uplift
and what it expresses. There seemed a pureness in this –

the source of his music restorative, liquid, breezy as cliffs.

MOSQUITO IN AMBER

Mosquito, this is where I'm glad to find
you, trapped in amber,
proboscis not able to push
into my skin. Now I'm quick
to admire your anatomy, flashy
as flying specimens I've recently slapped.
Head, thorax, abdomen,
perfectly intact; wings' immaculate crossveins
possible in the lit museum case to spot;
the compound eyes, feisty antennae –
and giant legs saved from parading
a parasite further into her prime.

But even better, mosquito, in spite
of our closeness, is the complete absence
for me of itch, swelling, angry rash,
guaranteed by the eighty-million-year-old
confinement of anticoagulant saliva –
making it dreamily comforting
you've been here to stay since the Cretaceous
unable to drift, primordially
whining, in and out of my sight.

MEDITERRANEAN TIME

The swarthy plumber who sets a time
to fix the taps never comes. Water
drips in nearby limestone caves
with less regularity from stalactites.
Church bells clang, now in a frenzy,
then once only and, much later, once again –
shuttered solitude now in silent streets
during the heat of the afternoon. In the shade,
on dusty ground, thin cats yawn.
Hibiscuses expose their sexy throats.
Should the plumber come, after
a siesta's done, he'll likely find
no-one home. He may later phone.
The sun shines hard on a limestone landscape
from which, block by sawn block,
the villages have risen as did – but how? –
megaliths during the Neolithic.
There's no division of colour, honeyed,
between what's man-made and the land –
the villages often atop the coralline
capped mesa-like formations.
They look down on tiers of ancient cultivation.
Olive lizards spurt in and out
of drystone walls – a species
endemic to the island after the sea
gushed into the Mediterranean basin
with cataclysmic swiftness.
The Romans called the landfall Gaulus.
Its stratified cliffs are the Miocene
made scenic. Marine fossils
in a fanned museum line up
under glass, put a contemporary shine
on geologic time; another case displays ancient bones.
Perhaps of a distant, distant forebear
of the plumber who, in this farrago,
shrugs off haste, short north of the cliffs.

ABOVE THE EQUATOR

What's so appealing is how like and unlike home this place is whatever the trial idea of it has formerly been. Here the summer skies are cloudless, week after week; at night, the flat roof is a becalmed ship to walk on, the stars as guides. Do we, as a species, feel so alone that the appeal of microbial life on one of Saturn's moons might provide us with relief? There's no requirement, if so, to leave "home" to summon exile. Some days it might be handy to guide a robot on a necessary local mission. Our moon has proved to be a disappointment except as a force. The rise and fall of tides here are small. Mauve jellyfish pulse as if in gravitationally neutral space – beautiful on a calm day; dangerous to dive nearby. The sting is the stroke of a lash in a sea that's cool aquamarine. The mark of having visited might otherwise come from remembering strange, trad music through curtains, from an old house, which stays in mind as lastingly as a tattoo – a scorpion or skull and crossbones on a swarthy biker whose wheels meet soft bitumen along a cart-wide street, like news.

MOOD PIECE

Hung out on the line by its tails,
the white shirt drips as if
a rainstorm has passed through it.

The sweat has been rinsed out,
now the shirt displays forgotten
weather – its outstretched

sleeves seem to implore
their owner and the hot sun
to rescue it from vertigo.

Who could not fail to see
how dazzling, soon,
the dried shirt's become,

gymnastic in the welcome breeze,
a model of appealing cotton,
baffling gravity, no hands.

THE QUEUES

Elsewhere queues are forming
faces eager, anxious, subdued –
it's approaching midnight or
perhaps 10 a.m. Many at length
will be turned away from the Alhambra
but not, mid-afternoon, from a cinema
in Chicago. Cold rain falls
or the sun repeats, hour after hour,
its heat, and the queues are orderly
for now, up to a point, and typical
like those which expected buses
in wintry post-war London, no-one
shoving (or conversing) – civil
compliance, far off in time and place
from a stampede for a train,
the men's teeth stained
with betel leaf, the too few places
already taken. Today
I queued, without incident,
to pay for groceries, so the fine
phenomenon is freshly with me,
the patience, the small expectation, relief
and, with time aplenty to reflect,
exposed mortality, personal death
moving ever closer, banal to all
other shoppers as an old joke.
To die in a queue might
it seems prove easy. Most flow
slowly, straight or meandering,
ancient human movement – will climb
the Great Wall of China, skip
modern Rome; approach giant telescopes,
drawn to outer space, equally endless.
Wend down, during a war, towards
a tight border-crossing or,
under a big sky, crisis food relief,
unless, like an angle of repose, frozen

gravity, a queue's noisily breached
as in a landslide, perhaps
a geo-political tipping point,
the screaming factor. Breaking news:
the tired, the tested, the trapped
of all nations think, *Screw queues!*
except for those in which each person waits,
remotely, that end up for them
where their helpful queues began.

MACHISMO

Love hit
Billy, the kid, hard

though it barely
slowed his appetite
for wild oats.

That is, his guts
felt like porridge.

Let's spoon, she moaned
domestically, in bed, and they dozed –

sorely missed breakfast
if they overslept.

The kid, a thin legend
in his own mirror,
was constantly struck
by her touch.

GRAVITY

Crockery slipped in front
of Sammy's mum
as she faced the bench –
cups, plates. Then,
empty-handed, she'd run
her fingers through dark hair
and swear. Earthquake,
well, something beyond
our knowing was happening, the smashed
crockery everywhere. Sammy
and I got far away, smoked
contraband fags, confided. His mum
scared him badly; his dad
could be seen in remote
places interviewing people
on the BBC, a floating
situation on the concave screen.
He wore a trilby. To Sammy's
mum the kitchen floor
must have seemed wavy.
She poured nips of something
into a glass, and partly missed.
Sammy shinned up trees, hot
for rapid action, barely stopped
till he fell or gashed his legs.
His mum paused as she leaned over
gravity's small vortex in the kitchen sink.
Sammy had two younger siblings,
witnesses, and a cat. When
Sammy's mum, out shopping, walked
smack into a glass door it split
her stomach open, down,
she gushed too much blood to live.
Sammy collapsed one day after school
from a heart attack.
His dad, in black and white,
had nothing much remarkable
to say into his microphone
when the sound was turned up.

THE SUICIDE NOTE
Public Records Office Reading Room

i.m. E.M.S.

That first Sunday afternoon
in September, the day
the doctor and the vicar came
and then the police,
you became incorporeal. Now,
half a century later
I read their names, associated
with a body, in pursuit
of their professional duties. Soon
you were everywhere, like the weather
and then, season following season,
I had no mind to leave
you behind; dreams, those
that afterwards linger, still
contrive to find you alive,
slender, hair greying early, pale –
as on the day I followed you
to frolic in a near freezing, clear
Lake District tarn –
but not, as I mentioned
to First Constable Reynolds,
without colour. Father,
as I formally called him
in the Witness transcript, was listening –
and in addition, I recall,
drawing on his pipe. Nor
does the First Constable impolitely
record his response to our pommy
voices, mine unbroken,
father's as if weaned
from the BBC, neither
about to break out
of constraint in the book-lined
study, like what remains
of a family from some gaol.

Did the First Constable sit on
the notion, behind the desk,
there might be something tragicomic
going on, an odd foreign
matter, before his sceptical
Australian eyes? This mob
getting off to a bad start
at improving their lot. He never
would be in time to catch
me crying. I confess, belatedly, I did –
whether or not the Cuban Missile Crisis
or a particular new sixties
pop masterpiece from Home
was linked. You, mother,
who till that Sunday made me
say my prayers and ask
forgiveness for my mischief,
uncontrollable in your mind,
could not escape the crazy
stigma, magnified tittle-tattle,
damning the mentally unwell,
exposed like weakened beasts
trapped for an easy kill –
could not forgive yourself
for the black trouble, in a strange
bright country, stalled for a while, now
stalking you again; another
institutional bed assigned
and ready, no getting away after all.
Perhaps the dislocation
ensured it. I've thought so,
ever since I was left
to do the talking, ever since
I learned of your psychosis
following my birth. So you wrote the note.
Then the taboo was broken.
Now I have before me, freshly,
the Proceedings of Inquest,
30th January 1963, a copy –
following my right to read it –

which, insignificantly, improves
my memory of First Constable Reynolds,
his pen and paper, though not the events
I could now better express
and extend his patience, therefore
best left, with the original,
in State storage. There it's been,
till now, terminally unrequested; ever
to be read by me at a future date.
But why so late? Not because of any
great foreseen distress when reading
in the Depositions what the First Constable
extracted from his cautiously
tractable witnesses – quizzed
the quiet husband and the quiet boy as,
later and at length through
subsequent decades, I'd persistently
want the truth, the personal history
however skewed by far-flung
relatives; get them eventually to blab.
Though I wasn't ready, even yet,
to find that father, pipe in mouth,
had already indrawn, like smoke,
emotionally damning evidence. Full
exhalation might have made
the young First Constable pale.
Nor could "Found dead in bed"
or "Overdose of barbiturates", the terse
words of the pathologist
find me lost for words again.
The words I didn't dare
to cope with are your own.
Those in the final note, that brief form
that prefigures bereavement –
the gravity of them never
meant for me to later read
or relate, in your familiar hand,
distinctive as the crinkled skin
on your elbows, when your arms
were loose in a summer dress.

Words the First Constable discovered
and, after father examined them, filed
away on the notepad page
as evidence. I leafed cautiously
towards it, then read
as if the ink was still fresh
and it's not too late to intervene,
came to my senses, and spoke
in that public reading room under
my breath to you, as I began to,
so long ago, beside your bed.
Until, when steady, I looked around
at others bowed over pages
and wondered what led them at last
to intercept the past, seeing none
were any longer young – clues
perhaps to old family cover-ups,
or even acts where, as typed
for the First Constable, there are
"no suspicious circumstances".

LUCRETIAN

The roof of the house has never fallen in
exactly, though cause and effect
are rife around here, gravity
especially persuasive.
                                   Someone's limping.
Seek to be calm; to avoid
disturbance – death (not dying) being of no great
concern – is the aim.
                         Athens is in strife again.

Crunch that apple, suck that peach.
Next year the crops may well be wrecked.

There's much to be said about the weather
when it's not benign, lightning
fracturing the skies, the more the better –
a gift to the atomist attending to the sum
of things, his mind detached from that tricky
sub-atomic mix within the orbit
of particle physics. Ungovernable
as romantic love.
                  So listen,
although nowadays we fill the Void
with noise, diversion, surface chatter
or still, unbelievably, some Almighty, beyond
nightlights the silence remains immense.

Elsewhere, between sheets, is another
place to tune in to the heartbeat
affirming a chance conception, yours, the best
unambiguously good news around,

needing only, to approach it, modest shoes.

WEIGHT

They loaded the ute
early morning – sunlight
after three damp weeks – the staple
tables, bed, chairs; books
in boxes, five years' worth
of reading condensed
into an impersonal, obedient
weight minus the rejects,
the dumped, the given away.
Clothes, utensils, CDs,
a bike, all there, all
contributing to the buoyant
relief of leaving – the drag
of habituation, its awful
sickening gravity, slackening.
They might have been about
to back out, drive left,
then right, then again left
to clamber into reverse
action only ten minutes hence
or, and why not, got set
to drive along highways
through open, drier country
two thousand miles north
across state borders.
Either would have provided,
in the mirror, a diminishing,
absolutely fine rear view –
as also for astronauts, rising –
clear as their relinquishment,
in spite and because of,
at the now abandoned kitchen
window, the exemplary
fig tree, each year laden,
then lightly speeding into leaf.

FLEXIBILITY
Bay of Islands

Not a catastrophe, this,
   since no-one, as it was happening,
      was then available, sedentary, local –

rocks scattered, cataclysmically,
   as here only forces of wind
      and water can shift;

or else some guy does, a re-assembler,
   with a mind to take an excursion
      back through geologic time, stop

in the cold late Pleistocene
   where the coastline now
      is not. Locked once into rock,

the photographed arch that abuts
   the sunny cliff – those
      who pass under it relying

on the firm fact that today
   its inherent collapse
      remains held in play. Everything

recommends implied
   signs for work-in-progress
      or in-regress – flexibility

any way. So, a fine location
   for bipeds to clamber about
      lightly, as it is for a flock

of pied cormorants, atop
   a remainder, sentinel rock,
      to digest their catch. Flexibility

also of tilted and uplifted strata
   in the stacked sequence
      of epochal seasons worth

considering slowly so to wonder,
   in effect – at a flexible stretch –
      what a needle sampling

the geologic record here might
   make of this impressive,
      windswept collection.

As if for the palaeontologist
   who to me confessed
      he was deeply into prized fossil

pollen, its music, trapped in layers
   beneath Lake Tanganyika; made refined
      assertions about proto-bees,

surely those making that low note
   a bow might extract from a cello.
      Though what aeolian sediments here

might express I'm only equipped
   to know hearing closely,
      via a flexibly cocked ear, the sea clash

with rock in this irresistible epoch.

New Poems

A CARTOGRAPHER DREAMS

In my dream the continents shift
  north and south, east and west, the uplifts
    from ocean bed to mountain range
are astonishing, a danger, as I focus,
  on shaky ground, my telescope.
    All this happens in a seismic moment. To get
the drift of this, think of supercontinents,
  Pangea, Gondwana, breaking up
    as easily as a lump of clay, the planet rumbling,
the consequences immense. It's so magnetic
  I need my compass. It's back to basics,
    after dark, with a sextant to fix
an angle on the North Star. It is bliss.
  There has not, for centuries, been any call
    for earthly calculations as big as this – not since
I dreamed of overhauling the medieval
  world map of Muhammad al-Idrisi
    on my study wall. I kept it free
of exonyms. I overslept. It seems
  I'm never far from work in bed –
    T-squares, dividers and protractors.
The work's my boss and, to be accurate,
  without it, awake or sleeping, I am lost.

REMOTE INTERSECTIONS

A raptor, way above the fences, sees
    movement in short grass a mile away,
        the somnolent town in the distance.

Soon, cruising on thermals, then circling
    high over prey, the bird,
        hawk or harrier, is a photorealist

of the skies, its binocular focus
    on the subtle tones in rodent fur
        and the fluorescence of scent trails.

A driver, when the road straightens
    and intersections become an event,
        sees a raptor, soaring, to his right or left

on the edge of his sight, a frequent
    occurrence as he eliminates distance –
        though thereabouts a fast car

being of any remote interest to that raptor
    is monumentally doubtful, as it eyes,
        with high resolution, a mouse.

WASPISH

If it wasn't for the sting
on the tip of my finger, I might not

have found their way in.
I shook the wasp off

and discovered its entrance
above the front door, an obscured crack

in the wall. I hid my acute pain.
But I wanted to settle the score.

How big was the hidden nest?
My finger bloomed red. Wasps

have a temper and a marvellous sense
of direction. Wild stripes.

They navigate by memorising
geographic features. When

I looked up, a number of wasps
were circling like planes

on hold over Heathrow –
the workers, most likely, not drones,

which can't sting. I prefer
those drones, though to tell

the difference it's necessary
to get close. I don't want

to be a pest, so keep
a suitable distance now

I've located their nest. Warn others.
Wasps have been victorious

killers since before Mount Everest
began gradually to soar,

are super insects, one of the best evolved
of all the menaces to us humans

at a picnic. Nevertheless, we're both
co-operative species

and broadly omnivorous,
and now, in this instance,

have in common, a house –
though about any assumption

neither of us need to move out
nor be massacred, I have doubts.

THIS LOGGERHEAD TURTLE
at Mon Repos

How heavy she must feel
now that, out of the sea,
she's huge in the moonlight,
one of the planet's
great navigators, her flippers,
efficient in the deep, now
forcing her great turtle bulk
up the beach, her heart
beating faster. The effort,
and her ancient reptilian head,
so like a fossil of itself,
wise-looking from its lone
submarine journeying,
solicit human tenderness.
Soon her clawed flippers
excavate a nest, fling back
the sand, last in a chain
of such preparations, here,
over decades. When she lays
her hundred or more eggs –
as if dripping from her
into the pit – she seems
in a daze or in bliss.
You, watching via binoculars,
see the genesis of risk,
the probability a single
hatchling at most will survive
to tune into the appeal
of the earth's magnetic field,
and thereby return here,
the dome of its carapace
slowly emerging from the sea
lapping this beach some year.

THE YANGTZE

Never to return
to the longest river
in Asia, travel for days
along a stretch of its narrowing
then widening length –
many years since
I set out from an old wharf
in restive Chongqing, a hazard
to locate the modest boat, time
running out. Time, doubtless
won't allow a repeat
journey, should I desire it,
time at a premium
or squandered and, knowing this,
now, I recall, where we'd
moored on the riverbank,
being in the streets
before the waters rose
and drowned Fengdu.
In my hand a bag of sweet lychees
I'd bought from an old man's stall –
one of memory's trick
insinuations. The crew
on the boat spoke no English,
their passengers, except one,
were all Taiwanese. We might,
but for a few words,
have been signalling
to each other under water,
were there visibility. Meantime,
we pointed to the bold markers,
high up in the valley,
that showed the mad
height to which the waters would rise
for Mao's emphatic dream dam.
For the time being
the finless porpoise was not

yet extinct; nor, for now,
the Chinese alligator,
river turtle or salamander,
sick from swimming
in industrial and human shit,
visible from the boat where
not one of us who could afford
to board it would have failed
to act on symptoms
of personal ailment –
the vessel making long progress
where peasants throughout the dynasties
swam in clear depths of the river,
free of traveller comparisons.
A current prognosis: bad
from siltation and erosion havoc.
Time fled in the twentieth century
with man-made speed
and its wreckage – the waters
of the Yangtze, early in the blazing
new millennium, set to escalate
the rate. No time, therefore,
to delay making for the wild
Three Gorges, the boat,
from which we all gawped
upwards, small in their shadows,
a lesson in perspective, precious
as a site birds of passage
need for survival. The sheer
limestone sides a backdrop
for the Taiwanese with their cameras
poised for each one
and only frozen moment.
She was like a rare bird
or a celebrity among them,
a beautiful distraction, lit
by her own energy, a focus;
as the beam of her smile
increased, the Gorges receded,
an enticement for,

possibly, all of Taipei.
Hard for them to see past
the woman's laughter,
she was bright health
sponsored by wealth, and
for her companions
an illumination. In the dark,
sleepless, my cabin light off,
blind to the river, I saw
as if from a sidewalk
the consequent enthralments
of power and greed, their glamour,
primed by the brightly lit cliffs
of a city, time's digits,
and, more clearly now,
squandered energy, its limits —
then, with daylight, viewed
the heedless wide river,
earth-coloured, churning,
that would rise in time,
at its world's end, to supply it.
At Yichang, that massive
generating dam, a pale
precipice, with its capacity
to influence the rotation of the planet
and amplify collective hubris.

THE WATCHERS

Only the gullible or others
passing through who look down

would be taken in –
spotting from the swing bridge

a brown fur seal,
slumped upon rocks,

sun dry, ailing.
There he looks gravely

like one of the last
of his kind, eyes shut.

Whoever runs for help,
if help is to be found, returns

without it. Pity fills
the minutes. This seal's

repeated trick, before
his audience falls away,

is to suddenly roll
into the water, dive,

and always re-surface,
erect as a whiskered vicar

eyeing astonished mourners.

MANY SEA URCHINS

No wonder sea urchins have survived
other species wipeouts –

safe in rocky crevices
they are a menacing sight

for exterior defence.
All those threatening spikes!

Voracious feeding on algae
occupies their lives.

Only resident fools
would plunder their predators

and let numbers boom –
then soon a marine

plague's on the move.
Nevertheless, their gonads,

as any gourmet will agree,
are delicious, smooth

on the tongue, salty and sweet.
I have a flint fossil of one

perfect specimen urchin,
transported in chalk cliffs

from the Cretaceous –
so well preserved it serves

an aesthetic purpose.
This was worth recollecting

after, in rocky shallows,
I'd carelessly put my bare foot

on a contemporary version.
The lasting pain from its venomous

spikes is for the brave.
It was at the sad end of a lovely

exotic summer from which
I couldn't walk away.

METAPHYSICAL

Where there's not a whisker
of evidence, there's faith in the existence
of a preposterous, personal God,

yet when I spotted
the astonishing presence in our house
of a long-tailed, brown, hopping
marsupial mouse — soon caught
by my hand for swift release —

and then later recounted this,
there was universal doubt.

AMERICAN WONDERS

The pointed conifers looked stark
   on that clear night, against a full moon –
in their shadow, my tent, small
   in vast Yellowstone National Park.
I could hear wolves, wildly attuned
   to that lunar phase, far away
in the mountains. Eerie but I wasn't
   fearful, sitting on a log, sipping whisky.
It was the geysers, the petrified
   forest, the hot ponds, I'd come to see,
but chiefly Columbia spotted frogs. Now
   I'd added them to my growing list
of sightings, uniquely those
   of a lone herpetologist. The frogs
are not easy to spot. Thank god
   for my galoshes. There seemed
so few people about I could hike
   wherever I liked and freely get lost. Then
find my way back to a track
   shown on the map, which led me
to the place where I dumped
   my pack. Heavy but I was thrillingly
fit for my mission and still had supplies.
   I lit a small fire, added stream
water to a dried Thai curry. It tasted
   home cooked. The aroma must have lingered.
The astringent whisky cleared
   my nostrils, like roads. When the moonlight
suddenly exposed, between the trunks
   of gloomy conifers, a fellow biped,
huge, and soon approaching –
   likely attracted by the food – I dared
not, at first, reckon on its height
   and girth to be the outline of a bear.
Specifically, a grizzly. It grunted.
   If I were a hunter I might have gone
for my gun. But I simply wondered

  at its presence. Then, passed by me,
it dumped its full weight, gently,
  like a massive sack off the back
of a truck, onto my tent. To show
  that I'd already had enough,
I sat my ground, called its bluff.
  The bear fancied my last supplies. Kind
of him to try to ignore me, a strong guy
  with a soft spot for frogs, who gets lost,
is easily slighted. So I soon tossed
  him westwards via a vigorous headlock.
His fur smelled like old socks. It was worth
  witnessing his shock, among the conifers,
as if this all was fiction. Under the stars
  he seemed to me like the double
of some dark personal trouble, overcome.
  The bear had given up, seemed –
on all fours, gradually retreating –
  not to be in peak shape, while I took deep
necessary breaths, unsteady on my feet.

TERRITORY

(Gymnorhina tibicen)

Magpies watch people
watching them – their sense
of separateness is shared.

Daily, there is a smart pair
on the grass, male
and female. They can hear things

we can't, such as the motion
of grubs underground.
They strut, pause

then strike, obedient
to gut hunger. Fly up, starkly
black and white, to be two

immaculately groomed
carollers on a telephone wire.
These calls clearly get through –

the park is theirs, entirely,
not counting other species
of bird (and people) toward

whom they are careless.
That's my assessment,
as an observer. At best I can

only guess where the magpies'
watched territory begins
and ends. It is possibly

somewhere near the border
where cross-species'
perception reaches its limits.

ACKNOWLEDGEMENTS

The writing of poems and their subsequent publication is for me a social act. Before publication, I have sometimes shared my poems with others. I have been fortunate to receive welcome responses from, in particular, Adrian Caesar, Sarah Day, Stephen Edgar, Jennifer Harrison, John Lucas, Paul McLaughlin, Tina Morgan-Payler, and Jan Owen. I am very grateful to them.

AUTHOR'S NOTE

Some of the poems have been amended and in each case supersede the previously published version.

www.ingramcontent.com/pod-product-compliance
Lightning Source LLC
Chambersburg PA
CBHW030517230426
43665CB00010B/657